BLUES, THEN AND NOW
(History of the Blues)

Frank Leanza

Crystal Publishers
Las Vegas, Nevada

Copyright 1998 by Frank Leanza

All rights reserved. No part of this book
may be reproduced or transmitted in any
form or by any means, electronic, or
mechanical, including photocopying,
recording or by any information
storage and retrieval system,
without permission in writing from
the publisher.

Crystal Publishers
3460 Lost Hills Drive
Las Vegas, Nevada 89122

ISBN 0-934687-43-9

Other Works by Frank Leanza

Music Theory for Everyone
Music Book for Kids of any Age
Arranging & Orchestration Ideas
The Technique of Modern Jazz Theory
The Golden Encyclopedia of Music Theory and Arranging
How to Get Started with the Flute
How to Get Started with the Oboe
How to Get Started with the Clarinet
How to Get Started with the Bassoon
How to Get Started with the Saxophone
How to Get Started with the Trumpet
How to Get Started with the Trombone
How to Get started with the French horn
How to Get Started with the Baritone
How to Get Started with the Tuba
How to Get Started with the Violin
How to Get Started with the Viola
How to Get Started with the 'Cello
How to Get Started with the String Bass
How to Get Started with the Guitar
How to Get Started with the Drums
How to Get Started with the Piano
Blues, Then and Now—Nonfiction
Jazz, Then and Now--Nonfiction
The Stand-Up Guy (Screenplay)
Justice is Served – Novel & Screenplay
Sizzlin'- Novel & Screenplay
Welcome to Las Vegas (The City that never sleeps) Booklet
What's This World Coming To?—Nonfiction

CONTENTS

Acknowledgments XI

Introduction XIII

1 ORIGINS 1

Slaves from West Africa—Country blues—Emancipation Act—blue tonality—field hollers—work songs—spirituals—gospels—blues pattern

2 LADIES THAT SANG THE BLUES 7

Gertrude 'Ma' Rainey—Mamie Smith—Bessie Smith—Memphis Minnie McCoy—

Koko Taylor—Ida Cox—Lucille Bogan—Sarah Martin—Alberta Hunter—Clara

Smith—Chippie Hill—Rosa Henderson—Willie Mae (Big Mama) Thornton—

Beulah 'Sippie' Wallace—Ida May Mack—Viola McCoy—Bessie Tucker

3 MEN THAT SANG THE BLUES 22

Charley Patton—John Lee Hooker—Muddy Waters—Howlin' Wolf—Eddie 'Son' House—Robert Johnson—Sam 'Lightnin' Hopkins—Jimmy Rodgers—Willie Dixon Robert 'Blue' Bland—Sunnyland Slim—Floyd Dixon

4 SONGSTERS 36

Big Bill Broonzy—Tampa Red—Leroy Carr—Francis 'Scrapper' Blackwell—Ruth Brown—Big Maybelle Smith—Willie 'Big Mama' Thornton—Victoria Spivey—Alberta Hunter—Valerie Wellington

5 URBAN BLUES 50

Boogie-woogie-Albert Ammons—Tommy Dorsey—Charlie Barnet—Andrew Sisters—Will Bradley—Freddie Slack—Arthur 'Big Boy' Crudup—Harlem Hamfats—John Lee 'Sonny Boy' Williamson

6 STRING, JUG AND WASHBOARD BANDS 58

Mississippi Sheiks—Gus Cannon's Jug Stompers—Will Shade's Memphis Jug Band—Jack Kelly's South Memphis Jug Band—Birmingham Jug Band—Robert Brown's Washboard Band

7 FIELD RECORDINGS 66

John and Alan Lomax—Frank Walker—Polk Brockman—Lawrence Gellert—Blind Willie McTell—Bukka White—Huddie Ledbetter (Leadbelly)—Muddy Waters

8 EXODUS TO NORTHERN CITIES 71
Washington, D.C.—Chicago—Detroit—Philadelphia—
Newark—New York—Arthur Blake—Meade 'Lux' Lewis—
Thomas A. Dorsey

9 LEADBELLY AND MUDDY WATERS 81
Big Bill Broonzy—Lonnie Johnson—Tampa Red—Robert
Nighthawk—Memphis Minnie McCoy

10 HOWLIN' WOLF AND SONNY BOY WILLIAMSON 86
Charley Patton—King Biscuit Time

11 SOUL 91
James Brown—Aretha Franklin—Otis Redding—Sam
Cooke—Little Richard—Elmore James—Lowell Fulson—
Percy Sledge—Percy Mayfield

12 WHITE BLUES (SKIFFLE) ZYDECO 95
Skiffle band—Jimmie Rodgers—Fiddlin' John Carson—
Rosa Lee (Moonshine Kate)

13 BLUES PROGRESSIONS AND BLUES SCALE 102
14 RHYTHM AND BLUES 110
Big Joe Turner—Bill Haley—Fats Domino—Chuck
Berry—Bo Diddley—Louis Jordan
Little Richard—Jackie Brenston—Crew Cuts—Drifters—
Moon Glows—Orioles

15 ROCK 'n' ROLL 113
Platters—Penquins—Jefferson Airplanes—Elvis Presley—
Chubby Checker—Bill Haley

16 1960s REVIVAL OF THE BLUES   116

Buddy Guy—Junior Wells—Stevie Ray Vaughn—Willie Dixon—Brownie McGhee—

Sonny Terry—Memphis Slim—Billy Boy Arnold—Johnnie Shines

17 BLUES IN EUROPE   123

Rolling Stones—Yardbirds—Eric Clapton—Fleetwood Mac—Jimi Hendrix—Beatles—Animals

18 BLUES TODAY   128

Etta James—Robert Cray—Billy Branch—Albert Collins—Jackie Wilson—Little Charlie William Clark Band

Artists and titles   135

Artists—Birthplace—Born—Death   137

Bibliography   145

Blues Societies and Organization   147

INDEX   159

ACKNOWLEDGEMENT

Thanks to Bob Zoch, Postmaster of the Illinois Central Blues Club for sending the pictures of John Lee Hooker and Percy Mayfield. My special thanks to two outstanding ladies who live and love the blues more than anything else. They are promoters and producers of blues concerts in a sincere effort in keeping the blues alive and the new generation of blues artists exposed to the public.

Betty Miller, producer, promoter and President of the Big Joe Turner Musicians' Fund in San Gabriel, California, is about the most knowledgeable person I had the honor to meet about the blues. Her blues festivals both in the United States and Europe are always sell-outs. She has provided several pictures for this book.

Tina Mayfield, wife of "The Poet Laureate of the Blues" Percy Mayfield, is producer, promoter and President of the International Blues Society and the Percy Mayfield Memorial Scholarship Fund of Los Angeles, California. She has received kudos from the Blues Heaven Foundation for participating in the 1994 Muddy Waters Scholarship Selection Committee and several outstanding awards for promoting and keeping the blues alive from various social clubs throughout the Los Angeles area. And special thanks for giving me the honor to sit at her husband's piano.

INTRODUCTION

It began in Africa and was brought to America with the slaves. It portrays a condition of depression or melancholy. It is often associated with sadness, sorrow, loneliness, protest, tragedy and sexuality. It is the story of the blues.

The 'BLUES, THEN AND NOW' traces its origin from Africa in its primitive stages to the present. It profiles the men and women that sang the blues and the importance of the string band, the jug band and the washboard band and the field recordings in prisons, in chain-gangs and on the plantations. The blues is a musical expression that depicts the hardships and sufferings of the African American people. Country blues or delta blues originated in the southern rural states. As the African Americans traveled north to Memphis and New Orleans, classic blues became in vogue.

The Mississippi Delta has often been referred to as The Land Where the Blues Began. It is located in the northwest section of Mississippi. Riverton, Clarksdale, Tupelo, Tutwiler, Houston, Glendora, Grenada, Cleveland, Greenwood, Indiana, Greenville, Moorhead, Rolling Fork, Philadelphia, Edwards, Jackson, Vicksville, Richland, Hazelhurst, Natchez, Laurel and McComb are the towns and cities in this area. US Highway 61 runs north-south through the center of the blues delta.

The Mississippi Delta has many areas that are full of blues history. Tutwiler, MS. Is where W.C. Handy first heard Charley Patton play his guitar at a railroad stop in 1902. Morehead, MS. is the place where Robert Johnson was supposed to have made a deal with the devil for him to become a better guitar player and singer, and for that he would sell his soul to the devil, so the legend goes.

Dockery Farms in Cleveland, MS. was the home place for many blues artists. Muddy Waters lived in a very poor shack in Stovall, MS. The gravesite of 'Rice 'Miller A.K.A. Sonny Boy Williamson is located in Tutwiler, MS. Clarksdale, MS. Is where the legendary blues singer Bessie Smith died from an automobile accident on Highway 61. Ike Turner, W. C. Handy, John Lee Hooker and Muddy Waters also lived in Clarksdale. MS.

It was in the Mississippi Delta where the blacks were forced to work on the docks, in the roadside for land-clearing, on plantations and as they worked they sang the blues. Often times making up their own set of words that depicted their sufferings and hardships.

It was the land that produced some of the greatest giants in our blues history. There were; Henry Sloan, Charley Patton, Eddie 'Son' House, Robert Johnson, Muddy Waters, Howlin' Wolf, Big Joe Williams, John Lee Hooker, Sunnyland Slim, Willie Dixon, Walter 'Furry' Lewis and more.

The blues however, were not limited to the men only. Women like Alberta Hunter, 'Ma' Rainey, Ida Cox, Bessie Smith, Mamie Smith, Big Mama Thornton and a good deal more were heard singing the blues. They sang about drugs, alcohol, prostitution and crime.

As the blues became more and more popular with the white audiences, the black blues singers began to travel north to Chicago, Detroit, St. Louis, Kansas and New York. They embellished their bands by adding additional instruments that included the bass, drums, trumpet, violin and clarinet. After World War II, notables

The blues as we know it today began as a merger between the African and European cultures. In its beginnings, it came out of the shout and the African call-and-response singing. This call-and-response adopted the three line stanza (AAB) that developed into 12 bars of music. The three basic chord progressions that came from the American culture are the I-IV-V progressions.

Further into the book you will be introduced to no less than 20 different blues progressions and the construction of the blues scale in all 12 keys. You will meet the men and women that sang the blues and the urban blues. You will read about the instrumentations of the string band, the jug band, and the washboard band. You will read about soul music and the zydeco bands. There are chapters on rhythm and blues (R&B) rock and roll and the 1960s revival of the blues in Europe and the blues as we hear it today.

'BLUES, THEN AND NOW' has pictures of the popular artists and illustrations of the 20 blues progressions and examples of the blues scale. At the end of the book there will be a list of all the blues societies in the United States and in Europe and the role they play in keeping the blues alive. Today, we see more and more new blues artists springing up and performing in clubs, in concerts and recordings to a growing group of young blues devotees.

The blues is like the perpetual flame that will never blow out.

1

ORIGIN

The blues is among the most popular form of music that is associated and identified in the chronicle of jazz. The general public however, did not recognize its presence or its importance until after World War I. In 1917, Chicago became the world's jazz center and the Original Dixieland Jazz Band under the leadership of trumpeter Nick LaRocca organized in the Windy City moved north to New York to make their first jazz recording of Tiger Rag, Livery Stable Blues and At the Jazz Band Ball.

From 1917 onward, blues became the dominant form of music throughout the country. By that time, William Christopher Handy, later to be known as the "Father of the Blues," had his "Memphis Blues," "Beale Street Blues," "Yellow Dog Blues," and the ever popular "St. Louis Blues," published. In 1905, Jelly Roll Morton had his first blues composition published, "Jelly Roll Blues," "Wolverine Blues," "Dead Man Blues," "Harmony Blues," "Black Bottom Stomp," and "King Porter Stomp."

The general public categorized the blues as music that is played slow and sad. The lyrics usually told a story of depression, loneliness, sadness, sorrow, tragedy and sexuality. The field holler or cry that played a major role in jazz was also an important element in the mood of the blues. Each black slave working in the cotton field, the rice plantation or on the levee had his own holler that became his personal identification. Hollers were basically slow in tempo, without a formal rhythmic pattern and were sung by a solo voice. The melodic phrases with their minor intervals gave a melancholy character to the theme. The exact intonation of the minor notes varies according to the performer's expressions. Often they are attached with smears, slurs, glissandos (a sliding effect between two notes) or any other embellishments they may create.

With the added minor notes, the posture of harmony becomes blue, which results in blue tonality. In most American black music, mainly in jazz and the blues be it vocal or instrumental, blue tonality can be heard. The field hollers, work songs, spirituals, gospels, minstrelsy and ragtime have continued on with the blue tonality sound. Many of our classical and contemporary composers have applied blue tonality in their compositions. Blue tonality is the lifeblood of our American musical culture.

From where did blue tonality come? Most likely it was heard first in West Africa. The exact date of the blues is unknown.

It seems that the more we investigate its origin, the further back in time it appears. W.C. Handy said he heard the blues in 1903. Blues singer "Ma" Rainey heard and sang the blues in 1902. However, the earliest form of the blues dates back to the early 1860s and was associated with the American blacks. The development of the blues was influenced by black folk music such as the work songs, spirituals, field hollers, ring-shouts and certain popular ballads.

In the early 1890s, blues were sung in the southern states in rural areas. These "country blues" usually had the accompaniment of a guitar. To establish a time period for the introduction of black music on this continent, we must go back to the beginning when the first boatload of Negroes were brought in from West Africa.

From 1619 onward, thousands of Negroes were brought in on slave ships and unloaded on the water front sites in southern states. Once unloaded, family members, religious and tribal groups were separated and hauled off to different plantations. The reasoning behind this separation was to eradicate whatever culture the blacks brought with them. But, what the plantation owners did not know was that they could never take away or diminish the black's love for music. Singing was their way of communication with each other. Further, it was their love for music that helped them survive the harsh, cruel and often inhumane treatment of the slave masters.

This does not mean however, that the moment the black's set foot on American soil they began singing the blues. What they sang while working in the fields was their own creative theme in their African dialect. Regardless of what part of Africa they came from, Dahomey, Senegal, the Congo, the Niger Delta or the Guinea Coast, they had one similarity in common and that was rhythm. The Negro soon began including fragments of the white man's music into their own musical expressions. And, before long a rich musical innovation was developing.

After many decades, this innovative process developed into the field holler, spirituals, the work song, the ring-shout and the country blues. Accepting the fact that the blues can be traced back to the spiritual or the field holler, then we may ask, "How did we get the classic 12 bar blues with its standard chord progressions?" When was it that the Negro became acquainted with the chord progressions of the Tonic (I), Subdominant (IV) and the Dominant (V) that has been the accepted harmonic blues progressions?

The beginning of the blues-singing period actually began during the Civil War era. On January 1, 1863, President Lincoln formally adopted the Emancipation Proclamation into law. Emancipation gave the blacks a new outlook on life. It meant freedom. No longer would they be bought, sold or forced to work as slaves. They were now able to remain as a free family unit. If they decided to remain on the plantation and work for their former owners, they would be compensated for their labor. They were free to attend the church of their choice. Their children could now get an education in schools set up for them. Families could live together in new homes instead of the slave cabins. They had the opportunity to become teachers, preachers, politicians and land owners.

The blacks were free to sing their music openly without the fear of the white man's punishment. Their freedom also gave them the right to sing and imitate the white man's eight and sixteen bar songs, along with their own hollers, spirituals, work songs, and ring-shouts. It must be noted however, that prior to the Civil War era, the blacks sang their various forms of music as solos or in unison.

Blues in its infancy was a direct descendant of the shout and the African call-and-response singing. Eventually, blues adopted the three line stanza (AAB) form that developed into 12 bars. The blues harmony derived from European music influenced with its blue tonality of the shout. However, the three basic blues chords are from our American music culture, the I-IV-V, progressions. These chord changes most likely came from our religious music.

Emancipation also gave the blacks the opportunity and freedom to develop their music comparable to the white man. A classic example of this is with the Fisk Jubilee Singers from Fisk University in Nashville, Tennessee. In 1871, their choir director, George L. White, harmonized the spirituals of the white religious hymns with their simple chord progressions. After many rehearsals with this new spiritual sound, the Fisk Jubilee Singers toured the United States and Europe with much success. They also opened the way for other black choirs to harmonize their repertoire.

Many spirituals were written primarily as a blues composition. They are; "How Long Blues," "Precious Lord Hold My Hand," "Nobody's Fault but Mine," "St. James Infirmary," and "Hold On, Keep Your Hands on the Plow." With the Emancipation in 1863 setting the blacks free in the southern states and two years later in 1865 the 13th amendment was included in the United States Constitution abolishing slavery. They both gave a certain amount of relief to the Negroes. The Reconstruction period following the Civil War and ending in 1877, gave another rise and optimism for the blacks. They could now participate in the social, political and economic issues.

However, in the 1890s, the southern whites found it very difficult to accept the blacks as equals to them. And with their stubborn and obstinate bitterness, they have incorporated segregation laws in their state further restricting the advancements of the black people.

In 1866 the first year of the Reconstruction period, the southern whites secretly formed the Ku Klux Klan (KKK) to terrorize the blacks and tried to prevent them from voting. The Negro however, was accustomed to violence and threats from their former slave masters and began fighting back in retaliation. They further stood their ground to protect their rights and freedom. Being challenged by the blacks on every attack and threat, the Ku Klux Klan disbanded in 1871.

A second Klan was organized in 1915. Anti-Catholicism and anti-Semitism were added to its white supremacy. After 1920, it spread throughout the north and south. By 1930 there was an estimated 30,000 members. It still exists in several southern states, notably Georgia.

2

LADIES THAT SANG THE BLUES

For some unknown reason the women blues singers never got the true recognition as the men did that they rightly deserved. Their songs were not as popular as the men except for a few like Mamie Smith's "Crazy Blues," and Bessie Smith's "Down Hearted Blues." The majority of the women did not receive celebrated status as the men did.

The ladies that sang and played the blues were as talented as the men were and in several cases they excelled their male counterpart. Memphis Minnie McCoy could play the guitar better than most men and often challenged them and won. With the women, their blues was the story of their lives as they had lived it."Sippie" Wallace sang about her drug and alcohol addictions. Lucille Bogan's lyrics were about prostitution and her craving for sex. Ida Cox reveals her weakness for whiskey, moonshine and sex and Alberta Hunter exposes herself as a lesbian. And so many more had to resort to prostitution, whiskey, drugs, cocaine and cigarettes to ease the pain of their blues. But, in spite of it all, there are those whose life story will forever endure.

Gertrude 'Ma' Rainey considered one of the greatest blues singers in her time. Her country style blues singing of "Lawd, I'm down Wid de Blues," was a big hit for Paramount Records. This was among the first to be identified as a "race" label, which was what black recording artists on black labels were called. "Ma" Rainey, along with blues singers, Bessie Smith, Ida Cox, Sarah Martin, Clara Smith and a few others were among the first to develop the classic blues style. "Ma" Rainey's 1925 hit recording of "Cell Bound Blues," with her own Georgia Jazz Band is an excellent example. This was followed in 1926 with "Jealous Hearted Blues," with the Fletcher Henderson Band. "See See Rider," "Bo-Weavil Blues," and "Ma Rainey's Black Bottom" were also among her hits for Paramount Records.

She also sang about topics that were commonplace at the time. "Chain Gang Blues," talks about breaking the law and going to jail. "Moonshine Blues," and "Dead Drunk Blues," were about intoxication. Superstition was revealed in "Wringing and Twisting the Blues." "Hustlin' Blues," was about prostitution.

"Ma" Rainey labeled as the "Mother of the Blues," was born Gertrude Pridgett on April 26, 1886 in Columbus, Georgia. At the age of 18 she married William "Pa" Rainey and together they performed with the Rabbit Foot Minstrels. In 1905, her blues singing was the highlight of the show. She later became the first black female to be associated with the blues. It was "Ma" Rainey who discovered that Bessie Smith had talent and took Bessie under wing. Gertrude "Ma" Rainey died of a heart attack on December 22, 1939.

For the major part, women were the classic blues singers. The lyrics were invariably taken from a woman's viewpoint. On the other hand, men ruled in the country blues with two outstanding exceptions, they were; Ida May Mack and Bessie

Tucker. It was however, the black female classic blues singers namely, "Ma" Rainey, Mamie Smith, Bessie Smith, and Chippie Hill to mention a few that brought blues to public notice in the United States. Bessie Tucker sang songs about prison life. Lucille Bogan sang "Low down Blues" about prostitution and lesbians. Memphis Minnie McCoy sang "The Memphis Minnie-Jitis Blues," that had reference to her illness. Later with her third husband Earnest Lawler backing her on guitar recorded "me and My Chauffer Blues" which became one of her biggest hits. It was women like these that took the blues out of the south and introduced it to the northern states, namely, Kansas City, Chicago and New York.

The turn of the century witnessed some major changes in the music industry. In 1900, the "Cake Walk" became the most popular dance. Ragtime jazz was heard throughout the United States in 1901. The Carl Lindstrom Company in Berlin, Germany, in 1904 produced the phonograph and phonograph records. 1912 was the year that Leroy "Lasses" White's "Nigger Blues," the "Dallas Blues" by Hart Wand and Lloyd Garrett and W. C. Handy's "Memphis Blues" had been published. New Orleans was hearing classic jazz in 1915, and in 1916, jazz took over in the United States. Europe welcomed the arrival of jazz in 1919.

Mamie Smith at the age of 37 made her record debut on St Valentine's Day in 1920 when she recorded "That Thing Called Love," and "You Can't Keep a Good Man Down." The record did not sell as much as was expected, but enough to bring Mamie back to the studio in the summer of that year. With the band backing of her five-piece Jazz Hounds, she recorded "Crazy Blues," a composition by Perry Bradford on Okeh Records. In the first month of its release in November, the record sold 75,000 copies. With the success of "Crazy Blues," Mamie Smith was responsible for the blues craze in 1921. The 'colored' market was discovered and record companies were recording as many black artists as they could get their hands on. By 1927, about five hundred records by black talents were released annually.

Attractive Mamie paved the way for other black singers such as, Edith Wilson, Viola McCoy, Sara Martin, Clara Smith and Rosa Henderson who began recording what was now called 'race' records because sales and promotion was mainly directed to the black people. The success of "Crazy Blues" made a lot of money for Mamie and Perry Bradford who promoted the record. It must be noted however, that Mamie Smith was not the first black singer to record. There were others that preceded her. But, her records were the first to be sold to the black sales market.

Mamie Smith was born in poverty on May 26, 1883, in Cincinnati, Ohio. When she acquired the wealth on her "Crazy Blues" royalties, she lived lavishly, buying expensive cars, furniture, the most expensive fashioned designs and a steady flow of lovers that kept her sexually occupied. She continued this life style until the depression.

In 1923, she recorded her last hit record, "You've Got to See Mama Every Night (Or You Won't See Mama At All)." Eventually, her money ran out and she found herself broke again. On September 16, 1946, Mamie Smith died in New York at the age of 63, penniless.

Bessie Smith began her musical career as a singer and dancer in 1912 with the Moses Stokes Minstrel Show. Gertrude "Ma" Rainey was with that same traveling troupe and had recognized the potential talents of Bessie and offered to help her along in show business. Bessie appreciated and accepted whatever assistance she could get, especially since it was free and coming from "Ma" Rainey who was the most popular blues singer in the south. Later, Bessie joined another touring show but was kicked out of the chorus line because she was too black. However, Park's Big Revue took her on in 1914. Within a short time, Bessie was the hottest attraction in the south.

Bessie Smith grew up in poverty with five brothers and sisters in Chattanooga, Tennessee where she was born in a small ramshackle cabin in 1894. Both of her parents died when she was eight years old. Growing up without parental guidance, she took to the streets for means of support. She sang and danced on busy street corners where people would throw a nickel or a dime at her feet. At a very early age she was introduced to a taste of liquor and sex and like them both. They soon became a habit. Bessie learned the street language as rough as it was and also how to physically defend herself

By the time she was 16, "Ma" Rainey with her Rainey's Rabbit Foot Minstrels took Bessie along to get additional experience and teach her how to sing with feeling and emotion. It wasn't long afterwards that Bessie left "Ma" Rainey and branched out on her own. She joined other touring groups working the black vaudeville circuit and in saloons and local theaters.

During all this exposure, Bessie was listening to the great blues singers. Besides "Ma" Rainey, there was Mamie Smith's (no relation) hit record of "Crazy Blues." Bessie was attracting attention with the public and several important ears heard her. Pianist and songwriter Clarence Williams and producer Frank Walker of New York were counted among those who claimed to have discovered her. During the decade of the 1920s, Bessie recorded with the jazz giants of that era namely, Fletcher Henderson, Louis Armstrong, Coleman Hawkins, James P. Johnson and Don Redman

On February 16, 1923, Frank Walker took Bessie Smith to Columbia Record Company to record her first record, "Down Hearted Blues" and "Gulf Coast Blues," with Clarence Williams on piano. Within six months after its release to the public, the record sold 780,000 copies. Sales were not only sold to the blacks in the south but northern whites were buying records. Bessie's popularity grew so rapid that people both blacks and whites would stand on line to see her perform. She was officially crowned by the public as the "Empress of the Blues."

In September 1923, she was called in to record "Jailhouse Blues" that turned out to be another hit. Among the classic blues singers, "Ma" Rainey, Mamie Smith, Sara Martin, Alberta Hunter, Ida Cox, Clara Smith and a few others, Bessie was considered the best of them all. During her ten-year recording career with Columbia Records with whom she had gotten out of bankruptcy with her "Down Hearted Blues." Bessie made an enormous amount of money. But she never forgot what it was like to be poor, nor did she forget where she came from. Bessie was living high. Buying everything she wanted without concern of the cost. She drank heavily and engaged in sex with both men and women. Bessie was rough, tough and often crude and irresponsible. Yet, at the same time she was passionate, generous and showed kindness to those in need.

She made one big mistake however, she entrusted her money management to her husband Jack McGee, an ex-policeman who in turn kept his pockets full and used Bessie's money to support and finance the career of his show-girl mistress. By the end of the 1920s, the blues lost its public appeal. Records were not selling. Theaters were closing down and those that remained open were not using stage shows. Bessie was back where she started. She was poor again. She had to sing at house parties to raise money to pay the rent and buy food. Her Husband took off with his mistress. All the people she helped in their time of need were not there for her when she needed them. The last record Bessie recorded was in 1919. It was, oddly enough, "Nobody Knows You When you're Down and Out," it was the story of her life

At the beginning of the 1930s, Bessie Smith made a successful comeback. Connie's Inn, a nightclub in Harlem, New York and the Wander Inn Café in Philadelphia, featured Bessie in a new musical revue. Again the public couldn't get enough of her. Bessie's spirits were lifted and she began to make lots of money again. Unfortunately, in the zenith of her successful return to the blues, Bessie was killed in a car accident on Highway 61, near Clarksdale, Mississippi on September 26, 1937. Richard Morgan, her latest lover and driver of her new Packard, struck an oncoming truck causing the car to turn over and sever Bessie's arm at the elbow.

A passing motorist, who happened to be a white physician from Memphis, stopped his car to render assistance to Bessie. Dr. Hugh Smith had called for an ambulance to take Bessie to the hospital. Twenty minutes or thereabouts later with no ambulance in sight, Dr. Smith put Bessie in his car to drive her to the hospital himself. However, a second accident occurred at the scene when a speeding car with a young intoxicated couple smashed into the rear of the doctor's car which in turn smashed into Bessie's Packard and overturned the doctor's car.

Finally, two ambulances arrived, one that the doctor called for and the other that the truck driver requested when he got to the nearest telephone. One ambulance took the white couple to the white hospital nearby and the other ambulance took Bessie to the hospital for the blacks about a quarter of a mile further away. It made no difference which hospital she went to, with her abundant loss of blood she died on the way to the hospital. She was 53 years old. The epitaph on her gravestone read; "The greatest blues singer in the world will never stop singing.

Many blues singers from the early 1920s came from the southern or Midwestern states. There was Gertrude "Ma" Rainey, born in Athens, Georgia; Mamie Smith was from Cincinnati, Ohio, Memphis Minnie McCoy, from Louisiana, Victoria Spivey, from Texas, Ida Cox from Knoxville and Bessie Smith from Chattanooga, Tennessee.

Memphis Minnie McCoy was born Lizzie Douglas on June 3, 1896 in Algiers, Louisiana, one of 13 children. By the time she was eight years old she was singing in the street in Memphis trying to earn money to live on. She identified herself as Kid Douglas. When she was in her early teens, she was touring with the Ringling Brothers Circus for a short time. Afterwards, she worked as a prostitute earning two dollars a trick to earn extra money.

Minnie took up guitar playing and learned to play it well. Big Bill Broonzy tells the story how she beat both him and Tampa Red in a guitar contest. He said "she was the best woman guitarist he ever heard." In Memphis she married her first husband Joe McCoy, a Mississippi blues guitarist and mandolin player. At that time she changed her name to Memphis Minnie. She chose that name because that was the city where she got her first big break in music. Most of her blues related to topical events of the day or about her personal life. "Hustlin' Woman Blues" tells about her life as a prostitute.

Her best selling record was "Bumble Bee" in 1930 on the Vocalion label. Her next record, "Memphis Minnie-Jitis Blues" makes reference to an ailment she had at the time. In 1931, she and her husband, Joe McCoy recorded an excellent guitar duet called "Let's Go to Town." In 1935 with her second husband guitarist 'Casey Bill' Weldon, she recorded the "Joe Louis Strut." Following this in 1941 was another recording with her third husband, blues guitarist Ernest 'Lil Son' Lawler, "Me and My Chauffer Blues" on the Okeh label.

Memphis Minnie was among one of the greatest and most powerful women blues singers of all time. During the midst of her successful career she augmented her band as did Tampa Red and Big Bill Broonzy by adding an extra guitar, clarinet and trumpet. Minnie's health was failing and she eventually died in a Memphis nursing home on August 6, 1973. She was 77 years old.

Memphis, Tennessee, the city of the blues, welcomed into the world on September 28, 1935, Cora Walton. When she was 18 years old, she married Robert Taylor and she became know as Koko Taylor. In 1965, Willie Dixon, a talent scout for the Chess label heard Koko sing and produced her first blues session which turned out to be a million record seller, "Wang Dang Doodle." From then on Ms. Taylor was crowned "Queen of the Blues."

Prior to her success, she had moved to Chicago in 1935 and was singing with the Junior Wells Band in local clubs. She stayed on with the Wells Band along with Buddy Guy until she got that big break with Willie Dixon. In 1975, Koko was under contract with Alligator Records and released her first record for that label, "Force of Nature." With the success of that session, she was invited to appear on several talk shows including David Letterman's show. Paul Shaffer, music director for the Letterman show employed Koko to sing on his album, "Coast to Coast." This was followed by B.B. King's request for her to appear on his album, "Blues Summit." Koko's greatest thrill came on March 3, 1993, when Mayor Richard M. Daley of Chicago presented her with a "Legend of the Year" award and officially declared that date as "koko Taylor Day." Koko is still recording and every one of her releases proves that she is the "Queen of the Blues."

During the decade of the 1920s, it was the women singers that dominated the early blues recordings. Many of them came from the black vaudeville houses that provided employment for these artists. Another source of exposure for their talents was with the Theater Owner's Booking Association (T.O.B.A.), where they would perform on stage in small towns and metropolitan cities throughout the country. The 1920 were good years for the black professional performers. Some were on Broadway in New York City, while others toured Europe with an all-black show. Then there were those that were fortunate to be heard by a record talent scout or a professional songwriter who had connections with a record company to bring them into a studio for a record session.

In 1920, record promoter and songwriter Perry Bradford was instrumental in paving the way for black singers to record. He took Mamie Smith into a studio and recorded one of his songs called "Crazy Blues" on the Okeh label. The record was an immediate success that brought in fortunes for both Smith and Bradford. Quick to jump on the bandwagon on Smith's successful record, other labels started recording the black blues singers. Columbia Records in 1923 recorded Bessie Smith's "Down Hearted Blues" backed with "Gulf Coast Blues," and Gertrude

'Ma' Rainey recorded "Bo-Weavil Blues" and "Moonshine Blues" for the Paramount label in the same year.

Mamie Smith, Bessie Smith and "Ma" Rainey were the first to be identified as the "classic blues singers". The 1920s brought on additional black ladies that sang the blues, among them were Trixie Smith from Atlanta, Georgia, whose record "Trixie's Blues" for the black Swan label in 1922, created such a stir that she, was called in for more sessions. The sides were; "My Man Rocks Me," "Railroad Blues," "Mining Camp Blues." And "Freight Train Blues."

Sara Martin, known for her showmanship and ability to please an audience, recorded her first record for the Okeh label in 1922 that became an outstanding hit. "Sugar Blues" was such a classic example of her talents that trumpeter Clyde McCoy used that song as his big band theme in the 1930s. Born in Louisville, Kentucky, she continued to record hits such as, "Joe Turner Blues," "Michigan Water Blues," "Blind Man Blues," "Hesitation Blues," and "Tony Jackson Blues." In 1928, Sara retired from the music profession and devoted her time to church activities.

Probably one of the most underrated blues singers was Ida Cox, born on February 25, 1896 in Toccoa, Georgia. By the time she was 14 years old she was singing in a minstrel show and was performing in theaters in her hometown. In 1923, Paramount Records recorded several hits with Ida, some of them were, "Graveyard Dreams Blues," "Any Women's Blues," "Lawdy, Lawdy Blues," "I've Got the Blues for Rampart Street," "Coffin Blues," and "Marble Stone Blues."

Although Ida was an exceptionally good singer with accurate voice control, she would always be billed as the "Uncrowned Queen of the Blues." The explanation some musician who had worked with Ida said that she was in the same time period of three black singers that have captured the hearts of the public, namely, 'Ma' Rainey, Mamie Smith and Bessie Smith, whose recordings have by far surpassed Ida's. Then again, Cox's music was of the morbid side. The lyrics that tell about the graveyard, the coffin, the death letter, the marble stone and the bone orchard, even her biggest hit "Wild Women Don't Have the Blues" appeal only to the women who understood the lyrics. In 1944, Ida was stricken with a stroke that put her into retirement until 1961 when she was asked to do a record session with saxophonist Coleman Hawkins. Ida Cox died of cancer on November 10, 1967 in Knoxville, Tennessee at the age of 71. It was the outstanding black blues singers as 'Ma' Rainey, Bessie Smith, Mamie Smith and Ida Cox who had fused the bond between jazz and the blues in the 1920s.

Texas born Beulah "Sippie" Wallace enjoyed her hits of "Shorty George" and "Up the Country Blues" on the Okeh label in 1923 and then again in 1926 with "Special Delivery Blues" with Louis Armstrong accompanying her on trumpet. The success of these records was short lived. "Sippie" survived by playing gigs around town. Then in 1960 she found fame again as the featured artist on the Folk Festival Circuit where she remained until her death in 1986.

Victoria Spivey was born on October 15, 1906 in Houston, Texas. She came from a musical family whose father was the leader of a string band in Houston, Texas. By the time she was 12 years old she was singing and playing piano at the Lincoln Theater in Dallas. As she got a little older she left Texas and traveled north to St. Louis. An agent for the Okeh Record Company heard her and contracted her to a session in 1926. The sides she recorded were; "Black Snake Blues" and "Deep Sea Diver." The record sales were high and in 1927 she recorded "T.B.Blues," a song about tuberculosis and "Dope Head Blues" relating to the cocaine users with guitarist Lonnie Johnson accompanying her. Victoria went on to do more recordings with the accompaniment of the musical giants as King Oliver, Louis Armstrong and Henry "Red" Allen. Her career carried her through the 1930s and 1940s. She worked the night club circuit and several tours throughout the country during the 1950s. Then in the 1960, her fame was renewed again during the blues revival. She continued on singing and playing her piano up to the time of her demise. Victoria died on October 3, 1976. She was 70 years old.

Lucille Bogan, born in Birmingham, Alabama, was considered to have the most scurrilous lyrics of all the blues singers in her day. She was an outspoken woman and had the backing of the city's black mob. Her robust blues were about prostitution, lesbians, drugs and alcohol. On stage she would set the mood for her performance, so that the audience would know what to expect. Her opening dialogue was; "I got somethin' 'tween my legs could make a dead man come." Then she followed this line with, "I fucked all night and all the night before, baby, and I feel just like I want to fuck some more."

From 1927 to 1930, Lucille was in Chicago recording for Paramount Records. The session produced "Alley Boogie," "Women Don't Need No Men" and "B.D. (meaning bull dyke) Women's Blues," both songs were about lesbians. Then in 1935, her uncensored version of "Shave 'Em Dry" was so filthy even for a 'race' record that it could only be sold as under-the-counter release using a pseudonym. Lucille also made records using the name Bessie Jackson, during her recording sessions from 1933 to 1935. She was not alone however in this rough and tough image that she portrayed. There were 'Ma' Rainey, Bessie Smith and Victoria Spivey who also sang about murder, rape, prostitution, drugs, alcoholism and lesbians. In 1936, Lucille Bogan was killed by an automobile in the streets of Los Angeles.

The 1920s heard other ladies that sang the blues, there were; Lovie Austin, in addition to her singing she played piano with her Blues Serenaders and often backed up Ida Cox and 'Ma' Rainey on their record dates. Lucille Hegamin was a favorite with her hit record, "Arkansas Blues." "Down Home Blues," was a classic for Ethel Waters.

Dallas, Texas gave us Lillian Glinn's version of "Doggin; Me Blues" and "Brown Skin Blues." Bessie Tucker's robust songs of "Ride and Shine on the Dummy Line" and a prison blues called

"Key to the Bushes." Alberta Brown from New Orleans, Birmingham's Bertha Ross and Cleo Gibson of Atlanta provided some obscure records. Helen Humes, although she later became associated as a jazz singer with Count Basie, was a teenage blues singer in 1927 Edith Wilson, Mary Stafford, Rosetta Crawford, Hocial Thomas and Addie (Sweet Pease) Spivey, Victoria's younger sister gave us memorable blues in the 1920s.

The 1930s came in with another wave of blues singers. Ivy Anderson, Billie Holiday, Mildred Bailey, Ella Fitzgerald, Teddy Grace, Alberta Hunter and Georgia White continued to keep the blues alive with such outstanding hits as; "Trouble In Mind," "Dupree Blues," "Your Worries Ain't Like Mine," "I'll Keep Sitting On It," and "Daddy Let Me Lay It On You." The 1930s also saw the death of some of the greats. Clara Smith and Lucille Bogan in 1935, Bessie Smith in 1937, and 1939 was the end for Gertrude 'Ma' Rainey.

Some of the blues women who survived the 1920s and 1930s began to include pop ballads along with the blues in their repertoire in the 1940s. Mamie Smith was among them until her death in 1946. Lil Green, the Mississippi born sweetheart, started the 1940s with a tremendous success with "Romance in the Dark." She continued her success with another hit written by Joe McCoy. Memphis Minnie's first husband called "Why Don't You Do Right-Like Some Other Men Do?" The following year the same song became a bigger hit with Peggy Lee's version with the Benny Goodman Orchestra. Lil went on to record for Victor, Atlantic and Aladdin Records. She toured the country with musicians like Big Bill Broonzy, Ramsom Knowling, Henry Simeone, and Clyde Bernhardt and with the Tim Bradshaw Band. Lil was a religious woman who didn't drink or smoke. But somehow, she was implicated in a juke joint murder and had to do some time in prison. At the age of 35, she died in Chicago in 1954.

The 1940s heard the sounds of Sister Rosetta Tharpe who combined her gospels and blues singing with the Lucky Millinder's Band. Muriel Nicholls (Wee Bea Booze) made a cover record of 'Ma' Rainey's 1924 hit, "See See Rider." Pearl Bailey, Sarah Vaughan, Camille Howard, Una Mae Carlisle, Savannah Churchill and Dinah Washington joined the ranks of female performers in the 1940s Their library included ballads, rhythm and blues and jazz. This began to have more of an appeal to the audience than just the blues alone.

Willie Mae (Big Mama) Thornton was born on December 11, 1926 in Montgomery, Alabama. In 1941 at the age of 14, she left home to go on the road with the Hot Harlem Revue. She taught herself how to play the drums and harmonica and she played them well enough to be featured as an instrumentalist on stage. In 1953, Big Mama Thornton recorded "Hound Dog" on the Peacock label with band leader Johnny Otis. It was an immediate success hitting the number one spot on the rhythm and blues charts. In 1956, Elvis Presley made a cover record with "Hound Dog" that became an international sensation. Thornton was a hard belting blues singer, similar to her idol Memphis Minnie McCoy. She toured throughout Europe and the United States until her demise on April 25, 1984. She was 58 years old.

Alberta Hunter was born on April 1, 1895 in Memphis, Tennessee. As early as 1912 she was singing in nightclubs in Chicago. In 1921 she wrote and recorded her first song, "Down Hearted Blues." Two years later that song became Bessie Smith's number one hit. On her recording sessions Alberta used the best musicians available, Fletcher Henderson, Eubie Blake, Louis Armstrong, Fats Waller and Sidney Bechet. She was a talented songwriter and recorded most of her own songs. "Chirping the Blues," "Down South Blues." "Experience Blues" and "My Castle's Rockin'." She recorded with several record companies at the same time using a different name for each label. She was Alberta Prime on the Biltmore label, on Gennett Records she was Josephine Beatty and for the Okeh, Victor and Columbia labels she used her own name.

She was also very active in stage shows. She replaced Bessie Smith in the "How Come?" revue of 1921 and alter starred in "Showboat" with Paul Robeson at the London Palladium in 1928-29. While performing in the Dreamland Café on South State Street in Chicago, she was billed as the "Sweetheart of Dreamland." She continued to perform until the time of her death on October 17, 1984, in Roosevelt, New York. She was 89 years old.

Ruth Weston, better known as Ruth Brown was born on January 12, 1928 in Portsmouth, Virginia. In 1945, when she was 17 years old she left home to join the Lucky Millinger's Orchestra. She stayed with the band for one month and decided to go out on her own as a solo artist. It was a good move for her. In 1950 Atlantic Records released her first big hit, "Teardrops in My Eyes." She became the top female rhythm and blues (R&B) singer. She continued to release hit after hit for the label, "Mama He Treats Your Daughter Mean," "Lucky Lips," "So Long," "Am I Making the Same Mistake Again," and "It's A Good Day for the Blues."

Ruth Brown has done it all. She was named "Miss Rhythm," won a Tony award for her performance in "Black and Blue" on the Broadway stage in New York City. She received a Grammy for her "Blues on Broadway" album. She was inducted in the Rock and Roll Hall of Fame. In 1999 she was hospitalized for cancer and the operation proved successful. Today, in the year 2003, at the age of 75, she is still singing the music she loves.

Bonnie Raitt, Hannah Sylvester, Viola Wells, Valerie Wellington, Lynn White, Denise LaSalle, Jessie Mae Hemphill, Margie Evans and Elizabeth Cotton were also among the great ladies of he blues. They sang about anxieties, hopes, desires and frustrations. They sang about oppression, depression and sexual behavior. They sang about gambling, drinking, prostitution and murder. And as they were traveling from state to state with the "Medicine Show" or the vaudeville circuit, they were spreading the blues to the public. They were the women who were called the classic blue singers.

3

MEN THAT SANG THE BLUES

The 1950s brought on an abundance of blues singers from the south to settle in northern cities. With the appearance of Charley Patton, 'Son' House, Muddy Waters, Howlin' Wolf, Robert Johnson and now John Lee Hooker, it seems that the delta has claimed more famous artists than any other region in the south.

John Lee Hooker, born on August 22, 1917 in Clarksdale, Mississippi, where he remained until the age of 30. In 1947, he migrated north to Detroit stopping along the way in Memphis and

Cincinnati to work in the factories to earn traveling money before arriving at his final destination in Detroit. While in Detroit, John could often be seen and heard playing his guitar on the corner of Hastings Street and Piquette Avenue where people would put money in a hat he had sitting on the sidewalk.

John Lee was gifted with a pleasant rich voice that was very effective on slow blues as can be heard on his "Cold Chills All over Me," on the Modern label. His first record, "Boogie Chiller" for Modern Records was an immediate success, which proved that he could do fast, rhythmic tunes as well as slow ballads. Initially, all of his records were recorded on the 78RPM records. But, in 1959 on the Riverside label he recorded his first LP (long playing) album. "Black Snake" proved to be a true typical session of blues music and was highly accepted by the public.

John Lee Hooker was an illiterate man who had no loyalty to any one record company. His Philosophy was, "if they would pay me, I would play." And so it was, he recorded with big and small companies. It made no difference if the owners were black or white. He would also use a different name for each label. For instance, for the Gotham and Staff labels, his name was Johnny Williams. He was Texas Slim for King Records and John Lee Booker for the Chance label. Johnny Lee was for Deluxe and Birmingham Sam on Regent and Savoy Records. John Lee Booker was also used for the Gone label. The Boogie Man for Acorn Records and his own name John Lee Hooker for Chess Records. In his career he had recorded more than four hundred sides that were released to the music buying market.

During the years of his recordings, Hooker had many hits; "I'm In the Mood" was his biggest hit. Others were, "I Love You, Honey," "No Shoes," "Boom Boom," "Hobo Blues" and "Crawling King Snake." Hooker continued to make albums and in 1989 he received an award for "The Healer" on which he featured the talents of Robert Cray, Carlos Santana and Bonnie Raitt. In January 1991, John Lee Hooker was inducted into the Rock and Roll Hall of Fame. He continued to remain active into the late

1990s. On June 21, 2001 John Lee Hooker, the greatest of all bluesmen, died peacefully in his sleep in his home in the San Francisco Bay area in California.

Sam Hopkins was born in Centerville, Texas on March 12, 1912. He got the nickname 'Lightnin'' while performing with pianist Willie 'Thunder' Smith. Their music was so fast and loud that at the end of each song, people said that they sound like thunder and lightning that came out of the sky. He learned how to play the guitar at an early age and decided to leave home and travel from town to town and state to state picking up some money along the way with his singing and playing.

In 1946, talent scout Anne Cullen for Aladdin Records brought Hopkins into the studio for a session of his original songs. From that time on, he was probably the most recorded blues artist around. Sam was a prolific songwriter. He could compose blues on any subject on the spot. Hopkins however, had no concept on the form of what music was to be. He was not consistent with his rhythm or number of beats in a measure. Like his counter-part, John Lee Hooker, he had no loyalty to any person or company.

He had written more than two hundred songs that included many hits such as; "Short Haired Woman" and "Big Mama Jump" in 1947 for Gold Star Records. For Jax Records he recorded "Coffee Blues." "Policy Game" was on the Decca label. "Lonesome in Your Heart" for Herald Records and for Folkways Records he recorded "Penitentiary Blues." Hopkins was not a smart businessman in the music field. He would go into the studio and record on occasions with as many as 30 of his original songs, got paid as little as fifty dollars for the whole session and then gave the producer or the record company the rights to his songs.

Back in Texas, Hopkins was singing on street corners collecting money in a cup or he would sing in local bars for free drinks. Sam was bitter against society and certain white people. In 1948, he recorded "Tom Moore's Farm" for Gold Star Records. The song was about how Hopkins and his wife worked for a white landowner that cheated them out of money and mistreated them. Earlier in his youth, Sam spent some time on Houston County Prison Farm for his involvement with a white married woman. During the early 1950s, he was on a short hiatus when the blues music lost some of its public appeal. Then in 1959, Sam recorded "Have You Ever Seen a One-Eyed Woman Cry?" for the 77 label. In 1971 he was involved in a car accident, but he continued to remain active with his brand and style of the blues until his death on January 30, 1982 when he died of cancer. He was inducted into the Blues Hall of Fame in 1980.

Guitarist Jimmy Rogers was one of the key musicians in the Muddy Waters band in Chicago. Jimmy was an outstanding guitarist and was often called upon to record and perform with other blues artists, such as; Howlin' Wolf, Willie Dixon, Junior Wells, T-Bone Walker, 'Sonny Boy' 'Rice' Williamson, Sunnyland Slim and Chuck Berry. Jimmy was born as James A. Lane in Ruleville, Mississippi on June 3, 1924. The Roger name was his stepfather's which Jimmy preferred to use. At the age of seven, he was playing the harmonica. At 11 years old he was playing the guitar. Jimmy gained a lot of experience by playing with other musicians that included John Lee Hooker, Robert Nighthawk and Snooky Pryor.

His musical idols were, Tampa Red, 'Big Maceo' Merriweather, Lonnie Johnson, Big Bill Broonzy and Memphis Minnie McCoy. When he arrived in Chicago in 1938, he began playing in blues clubs on weekends and house parties during the week. In 1945, Muddy Waters came into town and Jimmy introduced him to all the club owners and other blues singers and musicians. Throughout the late 1940s and into the 1950s, the group called the Headhunters played the Chicago area nightly. The popular band included, Muddy Waters, Jimmy Rogers, Little Walter, Sunnyland Slim, Elgin Evans and Leroy Foster. Eventually, they changed the name and it became the Muddy Waters Band.

Chess Records however, was interested in doing Jimmy's song, "Ludella" with Jimmy, Little Walter and 'Big' Crawford. The record turned out to be a big hit. During the late 1960s, 'race' records lost its public appeal and blues artists found gigs harder to come by. Jimmy however; found a secular job of managing an apartment building. For a while it seemed that Jimmy's music career was over. But, in the mid 1980s, "Ludella" was re-released on the Antone label and was awarded the best traditional blues album. Jimmy was delighted over his musical resurrection. He formed a new band and toured the United States and Europe. The band personnel were; Jimmy Rogers, Piano Willie, Bassist Bob Stroger, Ted Harvey (drums) Jimmy Rogers Jr. on guitar and harmonica player Madison Slim. Jimmy had made an impact on such notables as, Mick Jagger, Keith Richards, Eric Clapton and Church Berry. Jimmy Rogers and Muddy Waters are credited with establishing the Chicago Blues Band.

Early in the 1950s, Floyd Dixon was celebrating two hits, "Telephone Blues" and "Call Operator 210" for the Aladdin label. Floyd, a self taught pianist was noted for his barrel house style of playing and played the blues with a slight touch of jazz. Born in Marshall, Texas in 1929, Dixon moved to California when he was 13 years old. By the time he was 19, in 1948, Modern Records called him in for a session that turned out his first big hit, "Dallas Blues." Other hits followed such as, "Opportunity Knocks" and "Tired, Broke and Busted," for the R&B Record Companies.

Dixon credits his successful music career to Charles Brown, Louis Jordan, Joe Liggins and Ruth Brown. "Mr. Magnificent" as he was known was constantly on tour promoting his records. Two young artists who later turned out to be superstars, namely, B.B. King and Ray Charles were on tour with Floyd's band. After a four year hiatus from 1970 to 1974, Dixon resumed his career in Sweden and became an international star while touring Europe from 1974 to 1980. In 1984, Floyd was given the Billboard Blues award for his hit, "Hey Bartender." The southern California Blues Society requested that Floyd play at their

Piano Summit in 1989. And in 1993, he was privileged to receive the rhythm and blues foundation's pioneer career achievement award. His latest album release, "Wake Up and Live" on Alligator Records is truly an indication of his title, "Mr. Magnificent."

At the age of nine, Junior Wells lived in Chicago with his mother. He got interested in music and brought his first harmonica for twenty-five cents at a Rexall drug store when he was 14 years old. He asked 'SonnyBoy' 'Rice Miller' Williamson I, to teach him how to play the harmonica. 'Sonny Boy' played some notes on the instrument and then told Junior to play the same notes. Naturally, Wells couldn't play them and Sonny Boy took the cheap harmonica and smashed it to the ground and sent Junior home crying.

Wells got a job on a soda truck and was earning $1.50 for the whole week. He went to the pawn shop where there was a good marine band harmonica in the window for two dollars. Junior told the owner that he must have that harmonica but all he had was $1.50, and he would work in the store for the other fifty cents. The owner turned his offer down. When the owner turned his attention to another customer, Junior took the harmonica leaving the $1.50 on the counter and ran out of the pawn shop.

The next day Junior was in court with the shop owner. The judge asked Wells why he did what he did and Junior responded with, "I just had to have that harmonica." The judge asked Junior to play something for him. After hearing Wells play the harmonica, the judge reached inside his pocket and gave the shop owner the fifty cents and dismissed the case. Junior however, did not know how to stay out of trouble. He joined up with the Calumet Aces gang that went after other street gangs to start a fight. Constantly in and out of court, the judge finally got tired of talking to him and told his mother that he would have to send the boy away to juvenile detention if he didn't stay out of trouble. After pleading with the judge not to send her little boy away, Junior's mother contacted Muddy Waters and Tampa Red whom she had met personally when Junior took her to hear his music idols to act as his legal guardian. They took responsibility for him. Junior felt secure knowing that others had a personal interest in him, and he began to stay out of trouble and to develop his musical talents.

Amos Wells Blakemore was born on December 9, 1934 in West Memphis, Arkansas. While still in his teens, John Lee (Sonny Boy) Williamson and Little Walter gave him lessons on how to play the harmonica properly. Junior played well enough to get into Muddy Waters' prestigious band. In 1958 Junior teamed up with guitarist Buddy Guy and recorded his first released album featuring "Hoo Doo Man Blues." Junior became popular with the white audience in his night club and college appearances. There was a demand for this dynamic duo of Junior Wells and Buddy Guy. In 1966, they toured Europe as part of the American Folk Blues Festival. In 1967-68, the State department organized a tour for them in Africa. Australia had them in 1973 and Japan in 1975. They were an opening act for the Rolling Stones in 1970.

Junior's songs were of a current topical nature, there were, "Vietcong Blues," "The Hippies Are Trying," and "Drinkin' TNT 'n' Smoking Dynamite." Currently he's on tour with a band of his own and in 1993 he recorded his first album with his band, "Better Off With the Blues," followed with a second album, "Everybody Getting' Some," featuring outstanding artists as Bonnie Raitt, Carlos Santana, Brian Jones and the White Trash Horns. It was his third album however, that got him a Grammy nomination, "Come on in This House." Because of the care and concern with a troubled kid, people like Muddy Waters, Tampa Red, Willie Dixon, Elmore James, Otis Spann, Big Maceo and Sunnyland Slim who have helped to get his act together had produced a blues superstar.

Robert Calvin Bland was born on January 27, 1930 in Rosemark, Tennessee. He was destined to be the most influential among the best of the blues singers. Growing up in Rosemark, he sang the spirituals in his church and joined a gospel group called the Miniatures. In 1947 at the age of 17, Bobby moved into Memphis at the same time that other potential superstars did. To expand his musical training he would sing the blues with a touch of his spiritual and gospel sound at the Palace Theater amateur show and would always walk away with the first prize.

B.B. King took a liking to Bobby and gave him a job as his valet and chauffeur. King enjoyed having Bobby around. Then in 1949, B.B. King, John Alexander (Johnny Ace), Roscoe Gordon, Willie Nix and Earl Forest formed a group, so that they could perform on the black radio station WDIA. They called themselves, "The Beale Streeters." Through the Beale Streeters exposure, Bobby was building up quite a reputation as a blues singer. He took to the road with Johnny Ace for a short time. Then Ike Turner produced a record session for Bobby Bland on Chess Records in 1950. The results of that session created a demand by the public for more of Bland's records.

In 1952 the Biharis Brothers was impressed with Bobby's singing and took him into their studio to record some sides for their Biharis label. The session produced "Crying All Night Long" and "Drifting from Town to Town." With the success of this release everyone wanted Bobby Bland. But it was James Mattis, a Memphis disc jockey who got him and signed Bobby to his record company on Duke Label. By the end of 1952, Bobby got a "greeting" notice from Uncle Sam to join the army for the Korean War.

Two and a half years later in 1955, Bobby was released from the army and marched right into Duke's recording studio and record "Army Blues," "Lost Lover Blues" and "It's My Life Baby." It was Duke's new owner Don Robey who gave Bobby the nickname "Blue." Bobby with his mellow pleasing baritone voice produced many hits for the Duke Label. From the years of 1950 - 1970, he had no fewer than 36 best sellers that landed on the rhythm and blues (R&B) chart. Among his big records were, "Do I Have a Witness?" "Lead Me On," "Yield Not to Temptation," "These Hands (Small but Mighty)' and his first national bestseller "Farther up the Road."

In 1981, Bobby was inducted into the Blues Hall of Fame. Eleven years later in 1992 with the many more hit albums that got on the R&B charts, he was inducted into the Rock and Roll Hall of Fame. Then five years later on February 26, 1997, at Madison Square Garden in New York City, Bobby "Blue" Bland was awarded the "Lifetime Achievement "Grammy. Today, Bobby gives thanks to those who steered him in the right direction. They are, B.B. King, Sonny Boy Williamson, Roy Acuff, Tennessee Ernie Ford, Ernest Tubbs, Elvis Presley and Aretha Franklin's father Rev. C.L. Franklin.

Johnny Johnson was born in Fairmount, West Virginia in 1924. When he was four years old his mother bought an upright piano as a piece of furniture even though no one in the family had any musical talent. But when little Johnny sat at the piano and started playing with the keys, he was amazed and so were his parents when a simple melody came out of the sound board. Little Johnny knew from that day forward that music was going to be his career. He would sit at the piano every day and practice for hours at a time. After finishing high school, Johnny moved to Detroit and in 1942 he was in the U.S. Marine Corps playing in the band. When World War II was over in 1945, Johnny moved back to Detroit where he met T-Bone Walker who taught him how to play the blues on the piano. He picks it up quickly and before long was playing with the likes of Muddy Waters, Howlin' Wolf, Memphis Slim, Etta James and Little Walker.

In 1948, Johnny took to the road and settled down in St. Louis. During a New Year's Eve party, Johnny hired a guitar player to join the band, the player was Chuck Berry. That musical blend became the most popular band in St. Louis. The blend that created the magic was Johnny's jazz and boogie piano style combined with Chuck's hillbilly and rhythm and blues sound. Together, they created the new sound that has become Rock and Roll. Chuck Berry was contracted by Chess Records to do a session. Johnson joined Berry for the recording and the results were the classic hits of, "Maybellene," "Sweet Little Sixteen,"

"Oh, Carol," "Little Queenie," "Memphis, Tennessee," "School Days," "Roll over Beethoven," "rock and Roll Music" and "Johnny B Goode."

Johnny Johnson and Chuck Berry have been on tours together for the next 28 years. Then one day, Keith Richard invited Johnny to join him at a record session that produced his first album, "Talk is Cheap." Not long after that Music Masters Records called Johnny in for a record date that produced his album "Johnny Be Bad." Invited to play on that session were, Keith Richard, Eric Clapton, Bernard Fowler, Bernie Worrell and Steve Jordon. His next album for Music Masters called "Johnny Be Back," had the talents of Max Weinberg, Al Kooper, Buddy Guy, Steve Jordon, Phoebe Snow and John Sebastian. Johnny Johnson is still active today.

On September 16, 1935, one of 16 children in a family, William Arnold was born in Chicago, Illinois. At a very early age, Arnold taught himself how to play the harmonica by listening to his idol John Lee (Sonny Boy) Williamson. When he was 12, Billy met 'Sonny Boy' personally and was encouraged to continue to play the harmonica. A tragedy entered into Billy's life when he heard that 'Sonny Boy' was brutally beaten and died from his injuries on June 1, 1948. In honor and respect for his hero, Billy added the 'Boy' tag to his name.

After years of listening to the masters of the blues singers and musicians, Billy Boy, made an enormous impression with his harmonica playing. By the time he was 15, he was playing with Bo Diddley. Billy Boy was an immediate hit with the public. He further went on to play with Otis Rush and Johnny Shines. Billy Boy made several records with Bo Diddley and the most popular record was "Pretty Thing." Arnold left Diddley to record his own album. After making several unsuccessful sides on the Vee Jay label, he was dropped from their list of artists. Fortunately, the British group, the Yard birds heard Billy Boy's record and they made a cover record of it that was a hit in England. The Yard birds at that time featured a young Eric Clapton doing "Wish You

Would," "I Was Fooled" and "I Ain't Got You." Billy's compositions "Bad Boy" and "Don't Stay out All Night," was sung by Mick Jagger prior to his joining the Rolling Stones.

Billy Boy enjoyed the publicity of these overseas hits that gave him some recognition in the Chicago area. He formed a little band of his own but still found it difficult to compete with the likes of Muddy Waters, Howlin' Wolf and Little Walter for night club jobs. On June 25, 1963 Arnold teamed up with Earl Hooker, Mighty Joe Young and pianist Johnny Jones to perform on a show that was recorded for a future release. The success of that show gave Billy Boy another chance to record. Prestige Records took Billy into the studio along with Mighty Joe Young on guitar, pianist Lafayette Leake, Jerome Arnold on bass and drummer Junior Blackman to record his first album. This session turned out to be a big hit in Europe. Billy continued to tour throughout Europe for the rest of the 1960s

In 1972, Arnold and a host of other blues artists put together a show and toured Europe. It was evident that the British especially took to the blues very strongly. For the next 20 years, Billy enjoyed his notoriety in Europe. In 1993, Alligator Records released Arnold's" "Back Where I Belong" and an updated version of his "I Wish You Would." Both releases enjoyed a successful sales market. In 1995, Billy recorded his big hit "Eldorado Cadillac." Billy Boy continues to tour Europe and back home in Chicago. He enjoys the acceptance of his hometown audience.

Albert Luandrew (Sunnyland Slim) was instrumental in the development of the Chicago sound blues. Sunnyland earned respect among other blues men like, 'Little Brother' Montgomery, Peter 'Doctor' Clayton, Muddy Waters, Willie Dixon, Lonnie Johnson and many more by working his way through the lumber camps and the levee. Sunnyland Slim was an outstanding barrel house piano player.

Born on September 5, 1907 in the Delta area of Mississippi his father was the highly respected local preacher. At the age of 15, Slim was playing the blues in juke joints and house parties in his neighborhood. In the late 1920s, Sunnyland Slim took to the road. Traveling north to Memphis, he was sharing the spotlight with notables like 'Ma' Rainey, 'Sonny Boy' Williamson, and 'Little Brother' Montgomery.

He arrived in Chicago in 1940 and began recording immediately for various labels using a different name for each record company, which incidentally, was the accepted practice. When Sunnyland recorded his first sides for Victor Records in 1947 he used the name, Doctor Clayton's buddy. In that same year, Victor called him in for another session at which time Slim insisted on using the then unknown Muddy Waters on guitar. The name he used for that session was Sunnyland Slim and Muddy Waters.

From the years 1947 to 1956, Sunnyland managed to have at least one or two releases for each year. During his lifetime, he had written and recorded more than 250 songs. He recorded for all the existing blues record companies there. Following the Victor label there were, Aristocrat, Cobra, Club 51, Opera, Chance, Regal, Job, Apollo, Mercury, Vee Jay, Blue Label, Constellation, Sunny and Hytone. On all his sessions he was sure to use Willie Dixon on bass, Big Bill, Little Walter and Lonnie Johnson. His most popular songs were, "Back to Korea Blues," "Brown Skin Woman," and "Woman Trouble Blues."

During his illustrious career, Sunnyland toured the United States and Europe with success into the 1990s. On his last performance in a local blues club in Chicago, he had taken a hard physical fall that landed him in the hospital. Unfortunately, he never recovered from that accident and on June 4, 1995, Sunnyland Slim died. He was 87 years old.

Willie Dixon started his professional career as a boxer. In 1935 Willie participated in a boxing tournament and won the Golden Gloves Award the following year. Leonard Castor (Baby

Duo) a local guitarist got Dixon interested in music and taught him how to play the bass which Leonard had designed for him. That was the end of Willie's boxing career.

Dixon, born in Vicksburg, Mississippi on July 1, 1915 was destined to be a legend in blues history. During his early years, young Willie would travel aimlessly throughout the south and northeastern states picking up odd jobs along the way. At the age of 14, he got caught stealing bathroom fixtures from empty houses that got him a one year sentence in the work camp. After leaving the work camp, Willie was encouraged to sing with a local gospel choir and toured Mississippi with the group. This was his first musical experience. But he still wanted to fight in the ring. He was good enough to get four professional fights and be used as a sparring partner for Joe Louis.

It was however, Leonard Castor, who convinced Willie to quit the ring and put his talents to music. Dixon took his advice and began to seriously practice the string bass. After World War II, Willie was playing in a traveling musical trio. In 1947 Willie was the bass player with Memphis Slim and his House Rockers that was recording for the Miracle Label in Chicago. 1948 was the year that Willie along with Robert Nighthawk the former guitarist with the Muddy Waters band recorded his own song, "Wee Wee Baby," for Columbia Records. In 1951, Chess Records employed Dixon as their talent scout, record producer, arranger, studio musician and bandleader. Willie left Chess Records in 1956 to work for Cobra Records. Three years later in 1959, Dixon returned to Chess Records. While there he was kept busy writing songs for Chess artists such as, Little Walter, 'Sonny Boy' Williamson, Bo Diddley and Chuck Berry's "Johnny B. Goode" and "Sweet Little Sixteen."

That year (1959) Willie and Memphis Slim recorded "Willie's Blues," his first album for Blueville Records. In 1962, the American Folk Blues Festival toured Europe and England, featuring the duo of Dixon and Memphis Slim. Willie was always quick to give a helping hand to the young British groups. His "Little Red Rooster" was the Rolling Stone's first hit. In the early

1970s, Dixon formed his new band and called it the Chicago Blues All Stars. They spent most of their time on the road and recording albums for several recording companies. In 1977, Willie was diagnosed as having diabetes that required his right leg just above the knee to be amputated. This did not slow Willie down. He was determined to go back on the road and continue to make records. His "Hidden Charms" album won him the Grammy in 1989 for the best traditional blues recording. He continued to record up to his death on January 29, 1992. He was 77 years old.

4

SONGSTERS

During the time period immediately following the Reconstruction Era, a group of black American songsters were entertaining the public with their rendition of the ballads, minstrel songs, coon songs, ragtime pieces, dance tunes and reels. Those who played an instrument would accompany themselves. The non-musician would employ someone to accompany them usually with a guitar, fiddle or banjo.

When the second generation of songsters became of age, they combined the older selection of songs with the newly added blues. Many of them were called upon to make recordings. Among the first to do so was Texan Henry Thomas with his early black ballad, "John Henry" on Vocalion Records in 1927 who provided his own accompaniment on guitar. Following close behind Henry

Thomas was Frank Stokes from Memphis, a professional blacksmith by trade and an excellent guitarist. He along with Dan Sane another guitarist formed the Memphis duo and was known as the Beale Street Sheiks.

They recorded several sessions for Paramount Records from 1927 to 1929. Among their hit songs were, "You Shall," "Chicken, You Can't Roost behind the Moon," and "Mr., Crump Don't Like It," a song about Memphis Mayor E. H. Crump, composed by W. C. Handy who later changed the name to "Memphis Blues."

Walter 'Furry' Lewis of Greenwood, Mississippi settled down in Memphis in the early 1920s and was the musical blues life blood of Beale Street. He played with the touring W.C. Handy's band and whenever the tent shows would come into town. Among the black songsters who recorded in the late 1920s, 'Furry' Lewis was the most tireless performer associated with Memphis, Mississippi and active in bringing back the black music to Beale Street

During the blues lean years of the 1940s, 'Furry' went to work for the Memphis Sanitation department as a street cleaner earning fifteen cents an hour pushing a broom in the gutters in the same street his music was once performed. In 1916 when Lewis was only 23 old he was living the life as a hobo hopping freight trains to go in any direction the train was traveling. However, on one uneventful day while attempting to hop on a freight car his foot got caught in the railroad coupling and he lost his leg under the wheels of the freight train.

Being a womanizer, 'Furry' was asked by a long time friend why he didn't get married and settle down. Why? he re responded, "should I bother getting a wife when the man next door got one just as good." During the 1920s, Lewis wrote many songs and was often seen and heard playing guitar on the Memphis street corners for tips. At best, he was a master songwriter and took great pain in composing lyrics for his music. From his "Mistreatin'

Mamma," came the lyrical line, "I got nineteen women, all I want's one more/Just one more sweet mamma, and I'll let the nineteen go." Yazoo Label, "In His Prime" 1927-28.

In addition to his blues, Lewis enjoyed playing folk ballads. Three of his favorites were, "John Henry," "Kassie Jones" and "Stack O' Lee." His recording career last only three years from 1927-29 and turned out hits that included "I Will Turn Your Money Green" and "Pearless." However, in 1959 he was rediscovered by Sam Charters and began a new recording career until his demise in 1980 at the age of 88. During his lifetime he performed as a medicine-show songster traveling with the medicine show.

Jim Jackson did much of his work traveling with the medicine shows. Born in Hernando, Mississippi close to Memphis, Jim recorded "He's In the Jailhouse Now," "Traveling Man." "I'm A Bad Bad Man" and "I Heard the Voice of a Pork Chop." His biggest hit was, "Jim Jackson's Kansas City Blues" recorded in two parts for the Vocalion Label.

The issue now at hand was, who were the songsters and who were the bluesmen. It was axiomatic at those times that if you were black and you sang you were inevitably a bluesman. But the songsters took offense to that theory, contending that bluesmen sing only the blues, whereas, the songsters sang a variety of songs that included the blues. Papa Charlie Jackson admits to being a songster even though he sang the blues as did Mississippi John Hurt. John made several successful records for the Okeh Label in 1928 and was comfortable with the identity of being a songster.

Leadbelly on the other hand stopped calling himself a songster and wanted to be identified as a bluesman. So, the question came up, who were the songsters and who are the bluesmen. Blind Lemon Jefferson a constant companion with Leadbelly wanted to be remembered as a country songster.

Charley Patton was born on May 1, 1891 in Edwards or Bolton, Mississippi. In his early teen years he learned how to play the guitar. He was fascinated with the blues and enjoyed singing them as he accompanied himself with the guitar. He had compassion for the blacks and sung about their brutal and unfit conditions they had to endure in the south. "Down the Dirt Road Blues," was one such example of how he felt.

Charley was a very difficult man to get along with. He had drinking problems, an uncontrollable temper and was married eight times. Putting his personal life aside however, it was his music that influences such great artists as Howlin' Wolf, Big Joe Williams, Bukka White, Tommy Johnson and his musical partner Willie Brown. Charley Patton was known to be the first great bluesman that came out of the Mississippi Delta. He died of heart failure on April 28, 1934. He was 43 years old. On his tombstone it reads; "The voice of the Delta." The foremost performer of early Mississippi blues whose songs became cornerstones of American music.

Blind Arthur Blake, a songster who recorded over 80 tunes for Paramount Records that included, dance music, instrumental music, ballads and the blues. While traveling with the medicine show, one of Arthur Blake's hit, "Come on Boys Let's Do That Messin' Around," was the public's favorite for dancing.

Medicine shows were actually a vendor's means of providing entertainment to attract a crowd with the sole purpose of selling elixir that was supposed to be a cure for all ailments. These shows provided employment for the local songsters, blues singers, and musicians. It was not uncommon for blacks and whites to perform together on the same stage. The shows also attracted a mixed audience of blacks and whites. Jimmy Rogers, a performer, was popular among the black people because he did all he could to help them in their music and also in finding work for them in various shows and nightclubs.

Among the well known songsters were Dan Sane, Gus Cannon, Walter 'Furry' Lewis, John Lee Hooker, Tampa Red, Big Bill Broonzy, Muddy Waters, Sam 'Lightnin' Hopkins, Sonny

Terrell, Bill Williams, Brownie McGhee, Luke Jordon, Mance Lipscomb, Dock Boggs, Frank Hutchinson, Fiddling John Carson, Johnny (Daddy Stovepipe) Watson, Jaybird Coleman, Uncle Dave Macon, Roy Acuff, Hank Williams and Jimmy Rushing.

Mini-minstrel shows that travel from town to town often featured blues and some older songs. What these shows were doing was spreading the blues around. The blues singers only sang and played the blues. They were eventually replacing the songsters. The public was more inclined to listen to music that they could relate to. The blues gave a description of disasters, personal experiences, prostitution, drugs, lesbianism, gambling, alcoholism, and sex and prison life. The black singers revealed in song where they stood in society.

The southern states of Mississippi, Texas, Tennessee, Louisiana and Georgia have produced more blues singers and musicians than anywhere else in the country. Southern folk blues often called country blues, rural blues or down home blues, all had the same identity as that of folk music. As the blues singers became acquainted with the southern folk songs, they began to sing the blues lyrics to the folk blues thereby spreading the blues further out towards the north. Many of the southern songsters that came from the deep rural areas such as the Mississippi Delta have migrated to the ghettos or the black sections of the larger cities to earn their keep by singing on street corners and enjoying the freedom to express their sexual pleasures.

Record companies took note of the wide spread interest in the blues and began recording many artists for their labels. Papa Charlie Jackson and Blind Lemon Jefferson were among the first to bring rural blues to the black population. Jefferson lost his sight in early childhood and was constantly escorted by his friends. As a young man, T-Bone Walker would pass the tin cup around the crowd that gathered while Lemon was singing. Leadbelly, his closest friend was his traveling companion and Victoria Spivey would always accompany him at house parties. She would handle the money that he received as tips in addition to his wages.

Victoria was also very close to Jefferson, she often remarked, "He may be blind, but he sure knew how to 'feel' his way around."

Furthering the blues along on record labels were Willard 'Rambling' Thomas, Alger 'Texas' Alexander. Lonnie Johnson and Dennis 'Little Hat' Jones. From the Mississippi Delta area were songsters, Charley Patton, an extremely talented blues singer and Willie Brown. Tommy Johnson had worked with Patton on the Dockery Plantation. Charley was the inspiration for younger singers that would follow. There were, Chester Burnett (Howlin' Wolf), Eddie 'Son' House, Bukka White, Bo Weevil Jackson and 'Crying' Sam Collins. They all had their share in exposing the blues to the public by their recordings.

The recording and the spreading the blues were at its peak in the 1920s. But it took a national disaster to bring it to a halt. The Wall Street Stock Market crash of October 1929 put a stop to most record companies. In the early 1930s when the nation was recovering from its crisis, Vocalion Records teamed up Leroy Carr and guitarist Scrapper Blackwell and recorded "Midnight Hour Blues" and "Hurry Down Sunshine," both compositions became successful, just like Carr and Blackwell's previous hits, "How Long Blues" and "Prison Bound." Unfortunately, Carr died of alcoholism and Blackwell was murdered 30 years later

The 1930 continued on with another wave of songsters to promote the southern folk blues. Among them were, Peetie Wheatstraw (William Bunch) who was referred to as the spokesman for the poor black people. He often sang about their problems with subjects like unemployment, gambling, alcoholism, prostitution, bootleggers, and hitching rides on railroads.

James 'Kokomo' Arnold, John Adams (Sleepy John) Estes, was popular with the success of their Victor recordings. North Carolina's contribution to the southern blues was 'Blind Boy' Fuller (Fulton Allen) Buddy Moss and Blind Gary Davis. Fuller was accompanied by Sonny Terry (Sanders Terrell) a blind harmonica player from Greensboro, Georgia. They worked together as a team until Fuller's death in 1941.

It was Columbia, Victor and Okeh Records that dispatched mobile recording vans to the south to search out the many blues singers who were discovered as they were working on the cotton plantations. In many cases, much of the talent would have been lost if not for the field recordings, a subject to be discussed in another chapter.

During the 1930s, Chicago was the hub for the blues songsters. Reigning as king at the time was 'Big Bill' Broonzy (William Lee Conley) 'Big Bill' came from the delta area in Mississippi where he was born in 1893 and traveled north to Chicago in 1920 as a fiddle player. Broonzy learned to play the guitar so that he could accompany himself while he sang. In the 1930s, he was in the recording studios more than anyone else. In 1932 he recorded "Big Bill Blues" for the Champion Label. "Friendless Blues" for Bluebird Records was recorded in 1934. He sang "Keep Your Hands off Her" and "Good Jelly" for Bluebird in 1935.

Mid-way through the 1930s, guitarist Tampa Red had expanded his usual trio, guitar, piano and string bass by adding a trumpet and clarinet He was the first to record with a five piece blues band. His Chicago Five as it was called, recorded "Let's Get Drunk and Truck" for Bluebird Records. The song was a fast dancing arrangement which introduced a new approach to urban blues.

Although Tampa's 1928 version of "It's Tight Like That" with his trio, it paved the way how Chicago Blues would be played in the 1930s. The rhythmic beat of the song makes this one of the best city blues for Chicago's songsters to emulate. Along the same line of thought, Leroy Carr's "How Long, How Long Blues" also recorded in 1928 with guitarist Francis "Scrapper" Blackwell, was successful followed with the urban blues of "Blues before Sunrise" recorded in 1934. His soul-searching lyrics were for the benefit of his country audiences who would soon be boarding a train heading north.

Carr, Blackwell and Tampa Red were the main influences of making the urban blues a commercial success, especially in Chicago. Lonnie Johnson a truly urban bluesman recorded city titles in the early 1930s that exposed the feminine deception, "Not the Chump I Used to Be," "Beautiful but Dumb" and "Men, Get Wise To Yourself." Robert Johnson on the other hand took pride in emulating the music of Charley Patton and 'Son' House. He also became acquainted with the urban blues by listening to the records of Peetie Wheatstraw and Lonnie Johnson.

Robert Johnson was born on May 8, 1911 in Hazlehurst, Mississippi. He was the son of sharecropping parents, but decided that that was not going to be his life-style. There's a folk legend about Robert that he wanted to be the best guitar player ever and was willing to sell his soul to the devil. That meeting, so the legend goes took place at mid-night at the Mississippi crossroads.

In time he learned to master his guitar playing ability. He was able to do things with the guitar easily that other guitarist found difficult to do. Robert traveled throughout Mississippi and Arkansas and played in every juke joint along the way. His first recording on the Vocalion Label was "Terraplane Blues" which became an immediate success. He died from poison by a jealous husband of a woman he was entertaining with on August 13, 1938 in Greenwood, Mississippi. He was only 27 years old. On January 23, 1986, Robert Johnson was inducted into the Rock and Roll Hall of Fame.

Joseph Vernon (Big Joe) Turner of Kansas City, Missouri was born on May 18, 1911 was listed among the main influences on the blues after World War II. Known as the "Singing Bartender" where he got his start working in Kansas City clubs. So impressive was his singing that he went on the road with the big bands of Bennie Morton, Andy Kirk, and Count Basie singing his style of the urban blues. Turner was a loud, forceful 'shouter' but his 1943 Decca record of "Lucille" gave evidence that he could also sing a sentimental song.

'Big Joe' Turner was kept busy for the next two decades traveling with bands and small somewhat like jazz groups, that complimented his jazz-blues. "Old Piney Brown is Gone" for Swing-Time Records in 1949 was reminiscent of his hometown of Kansas City. His 1954 Atlantic release of "Shake Rattle and Roll" was the doorway to Rock and Roll. 'Big Joe' Turner died in Inglewood, California on November 24, 1985. He was 74 years old.

Columbia, Victor, Decca, Vocalion and Okeh Record companies had the monopoly in the recording industry. But after World War II, smaller black owned companies began to branch out in the south and the west coast. Blues by nature, has always been considered as black music. All their recordings were listed as 'race' records, segregating them from records of the white artists. Then on June 25, 1949, Billboard magazine officially suspended the term 'race' and replaced it with rhythm and blues. The new term rhythm and blues (R&B) can now be applied to all forms of black recordings, folk, jazz, pop, or big bands. This transformation was in the making in New York in the early 1940s, then in Los Angeles around 1945, with Chicago, Cincinnati, Houston and Newark following by the end of the decade.

Louis Jordon, known as the "Father of Rhythm and Blues" made a million record seller with his "Choo Choo Ch'Boogie" in 1946. Louis was also the originator of 'Jive' music or 'good times' music. The lyrics are usually witty or insinuating as some of his titles will indicate," Let The Good Times Roll," The Chick's Too Young to Fry," "Who Put the Benzedrine In Mrs. Murphy's Ovaltine?."

T-Bone Walker was born in Linden, Texas in 1910. He joined the Les Hite big band and recorded some of his urban blues, "I Wonder Why She Don't Write to Me," "I Love My Baby" and "T-Bone Blues." Walker was a main attraction for the Les Hite band and together they grew in popularity. In 1950, Imperial Records signed T-Bone to a four year contract and recorded several sides. There were; "Pony Tail," "Hard Way," "Yes, Got a Teenaged Baby, She Likes to Wear Her Sloppy Joes" and "Bobby Sox Blues," which was later revised as "Sweet Little Sixteen" for Chuck Berry. In 1975, T-Bone died of pneumonia in Los Angeles, California. He was 65 years old.

McKinley Morganfield (Muddy Waters) was born on April 4, 1915 in Rolling Folk, Mississippi in the Mississippi delta area. At the young age of seven or eight he taught himself how to play the harmonica. At the age of 17, he learned to play the guitar. He emulated the sounds and techniques of 'Son' House and Robert Johnson. In 1947 Muddy recorded his urban blues of "I Can't Be Satisfied" and "I Feel like Going Home," for the Aristocrat label. Over the tears Muddy recorded many hits, "Got My Mojo Working," "I Just Want to Make Love to You," "She's nineteen years old," and "I'm Ready." Muddy's final public appearance was at an Eric Clapton show in 1982 when he was stricken with a heart attack and died on April 30, 1983. He was 68 years old. In appreciation to his contribution to the blues, the City of Chicago renamed East 43rd Street to Muddy Waters Drive on August 2, 1985. In 1988, Clarksdale, Mississippi declares April 21, as McKinley "Muddy Waters" Morganfield as "Appreciation Day." On September 1, 2000, Muddy Waters was inducted into the Rock and Roll Hall of Fame

During this time period of the late 1940s, bluesmen Sam 'Lightnin' Hopkins, Charles Brown, Frankie Lee Sims, Jimmy Rogers and John Lee Hooker were also working the nightclubs and concert tours. Women songsters were gaining in popularity during the 1940s and 50s. Ruth Brown, 'Big Maybelle' Smith and Willie 'Big Mama' Thornton were among them. Joining the women were Clarence 'Gatemouth' Brown, Eddie 'Mister Cleanhead' Vinson, Roy 'Professor Longhair' Byrd and Roy Brown. All of their recordings from 1949 through the 1950s were listed on the rhythm and blues charts. With this generation of songster's recordings, their attention was aimed at the teenage record buyers. Both blacks and whites would flock to the local theater or concert hall to hear them sing in person.

"Doo-Wop" groups began to emerge from the street corners and stoops of all major cities that became part of the rhythm and blues sound in the 1950s. There were, The Drifters, The Penquins and the Harptones. Talent scouts were canvassing schoolyards, public parks, subway stations, tenement hallways, front stoops and amateur contests for potential artists.

'Little Walter' Jacobs from Alexandria, Louisiana in 1930 was an accomplished harmonica player by the time he was eight years old. In his teen years, he traveled north and settled in Chicago by 1947. There he recorded "Ora Nelle Blues." In 1952, he sang "Mean Old World" for Checker Records and Bluelights in 1954 with Robert Lockwood playing guitar

Chester Arthur (Howlin' Wolf) Burnett was born on June 10, 1910 on a plantation in West Point, Mississippi. Howlin' was a big man, 6'3" and 300 pounds with a rough gravelly voice. At Times he would enter the stage on his hands and knees and howl like a wolf, ergo, the nickname Howlin' Wolf. He is credited with some fine recordings, "Spoonful," "Back Door Man," "Killing Floor" and "Smokestack Lightning." The Rolling Stones and Eric Clapton were influenced with Howlin's performance. His last engagement was with B.B. King. He died from kidney failure on January 10, 1976 at the age of 66. In 1991 he was inducted into the Rock and Roll Hall of Fame.

B.B. King was appearing on the WDIA Radio Station with the Joe Hill Louis band in 1951. The station's management recognized his talent and offered him his own show on what was called the "Mother Station of the Negro" The show created a demand for the public to hear and see more of B.B. King. In 1951, he recorded "B.B. Blue." "Three O'clock Blues and "Boogie Boogie Woman" were recorded in 1952. There was no stopping

King. He took to the road in 1954 and in the first year of his tours, he earned close to a quarter of a million dollars.

Record companies were eager to expose their 'star' singers where over 200 clubs came alive on Chicago's south side. Bobby 'Blue' Bland, Little Junior Parker, Jimmy Reed, Eddie Taylor, Buddy Guy and Sam 'Magic Sam' Maghett were heard nightly in one club or another. Chicago became the reservoir of black talent. Music from pool halls, taverns and nightclubs would flood the streets. You could hear Mamie Smith singing "Crazy Blues" or Louis Armstrong's trumpet blaring "Struttin' with Some Barbecue." Alberta Hunter often worked at Dago Frank's nightclub that was a hangout for pimps and prostitutes. Blind Arvella Gray would find his corner on lively Maxwell Street playing his guitar. Valerie Willington was a permanent fixture at Brady's Blues Lounge located at 47th Street and Martin L. King Drive.

Big Joe Williams was born on October 16, 1903 in Crawford, Mississippi. He was raised in the Mississippi Delta and was respected as a fine guitar player and singer. In the early 1930s he began his recording career making hit records that kept him in the studio until his demise in 1982. His big hit was a song he had written, "Please Baby Don't Go." In his early years, Big Joe traveled throughout the south hopping freight trains playing in juke joints and had spent some time in jail. He later joins the Birmington Jug Band and traveled with the Rabbit Foot Minstrels Revue. In 1941, Williams recorded another hit record, "Crawlin' King Snake." During the decade of the '60s, he toured Europe with the American Folk Blues Festival and in 1974 he toured throughout Japan. Big Joe Williams died on December 17, 1982 In 1992, he was inducted into the Blues Foundation's Hall of Fame.

Eddie James "Son" House was born on March 21, 1902 in Riverton, Mississippi. He was a popular bluesman that came out of the Mississippi Delta. In 1930, "Son" recorded "My Black Mama," "Preachin' the Blues, and "Dry Spell Blues." He later teamed up with his best friend Willie Brown and together they traveled and played every juke joint they came upon. When his partner, Willie Brown died, "Son" took his death hard. He gave up his blues life and quit playing and singing. After some time had passed, Al Wilson of Canned Heat convinced "Son" to resume his blues life again. On his return to the stage, "Son" was better than ever. He played and sang with feeling and emotion. Eddie James "Son" House died on October 19, 1988. He was 86 years old.

Booker T. Washington White, commonly known as Bukka White was born on November 12, 1909 in Houston, Mississippi. He was another one of the great blues men that came from the Mississippi delta. Being an ex-boxer, he led a hard life. But on stage during his performances he enjoyed the limelight and the attention from his audiences. He had an active career playing in colleges and coffee houses and traveling with the American Folk Life Festival tours. In 1940 Bukka recorded two hits on the Vocalion Label, So Help Me God," and "I Got Down to It." White remained active until his death on February 26, 1977 in Memphis, Tennessee. He was 68 years old.

John Estes was born on January 25, 1904 in Ripley, Tennessee. In the early 1920s, Estes along with Yank Rachell a mandolin player and Hammie Nixon a harmonica and jug player joined a jug band in Memphis. John a fine singer and guitarist got the nickname 'Sleepy' because he was constantly taking naps. In 1929 he got a recording contract with Victor Records and recorded several sides.

During the early 1930s, he moved to Chicago and started to record for Decca Records. In 1940, 'Sleepy' John recorded "Someday, Baby" for the Bluebird Label. The song was his first big hit. With the success of that record John moved back to his hometown in Tennessee. In the early 1950s, Estes became totally blind and lost all interest in singing and playing the guitar.

After living in poverty for more than ten years, 'Sleepy; John Estes was convinced by his fellow musicians to re-activate his career again. The results were great. He appeared in two documentaries, "Citizen South, Citizen North," in 1962 and "The Blues" in 1963. For the Delmark Label he recorded the album "The Legend of 'Sleep' John Estes. He began performing in concerts, nightclubs and the blues festivals. His career was soaring. He traveled with the Newport Folk Festival, the American Folk Blues Festival and the Ann Arbor Blues Festival. During the 1970s, 'Sleepy' was on tour in Europe and Japan. He died in 1977 at the age of 73.

Lemon Jefferson was born in Couchman, Texas in 1897. He was born blind at birth. With his guitar, Jefferson could always be heard singing on street corners in his hometown. During the 1920s he established a reputation as being among the most popular blues recording artist. His records on the Paramount Label were big sellers to the buying public both in the United States and Europe. Some of his successful records were, "Long Lonesome Blues," "Shuckin' Sugar Blues," "Jack O'Diamond Blues," and "Blind Lemon's Penitentiary Blues."

He was an inspiration for many of the young black musicians growing up to become a part of the blues era. Many of them tried to emulate his style of playing but soon found it more difficult than they imagined. Leadbelly, a competent musician was a constant traveling companion with Jefferson. Together they toured the Mississippi Delta and Memphis. It was in Chicago in 1930 that Blind Lemon Jefferson died. However, it was Jefferson's desire to be buried in his home state of Texas. His good friend pianist Will Ezell brought the body back home and buried him in Wortham, Texas. The inscription on his headstone reads; "Lord, its one kind favor I'll ask of you. See that my grave is kept clean." He was 33 years old

In the midst of all this activity were model T's, Studebakers, Buicks and streetcars clanging through the traffic. Horse driven buggies were dodging around streetcars, and people were coming and going from every direction. This was Bronze town, the center of the black community.

5

URBAN BLUES

Boogie-woogie was in vogue again. Boogie pianist Pete Johnson recorded "Goin' Away Blues" on the Vocalion Label. Blue Note 4, recorded "Chicago in Mind" by Albert Ammons. Tommy Dorsey and his orchestra recorded "Boogie-Woogie" on Victor Records in 1938. Charlie Barnet's orchestra recorded "Scrub Me Mama with a Boogie Beat" in 1940 on the Bluebird Label. Columbia Records released "Boogie-Woogie Conga" by Will Bradley in 1942 and Count Basie's "Basie's Boogie" in 1941 on the Okeh Label.

During the World War II years, boogie-woogie was still going strong. There was Freddie Slack's hit of "Cow Cow Boogie" with Ella Mae Morse. Will Bradley followed up with another hit with "Beat Me, Daddy, Eight to the Bar," and the immortal

Andrew Sister's hit of "Boogie-Woogie Bugle Boy." Boogie-woogie was so widely accepted by the public that it became a standard feature of the blues. Helping to keep the blues alive were, 'Big Bill' Broonzy (William Lee Conley), John Lee (Sonny Boy) Williamson, Blind John Davis, 'Big Maceo' (Major Merriweather), 'Little Brother' Montgomery and Joe Turner.

When the decade of the 1930s began, Leroy Carr, a popular urban blues singer and pianist from Nashville, Tennessee with his partner guitarist Scrapper Blackwell made several hits on the Vocalion Label, they included, "How Long, How Long Blues, " Midnight Hour Blues," "Hurry Down Sunshine" and "Prison Bound." Unfortunately, Leroy's career was cut short on April 28, 1935 when he died of cirrhosis of the liver. He was 30 years old.

His music was an inspiration to other blues singers that even after his death other artists were recording his songs and imitating his easy going melancholy style. St. Louis' pianist Walter Davis and Bumble Bee Slim (Amos Easton) along with Roosevelt Sykes, 'Little Brother' Montgomery and Peetie Wheatstraw who refers to himself as being the 'High Sheriff from Hell' were among Leroy Carr's admirers.

In the beginning of 1930, a time when the nation was trying to recover from its financial disaster, the lyrics of the blues singers were cynical and contemptuous. They were expressing their feelings about the Depression and the conditions they had to endure because of it. Peetie Wheatstraw (William Bunch) from Ripley, Tennessee sang about gamblers, prostitutes and bootleggers as his hit on Vocalion Label, "Kidnapper's Blues" would indicate. He was a favorite among the black people because he was singing about their problems.

When Franklin Delano Roosevelt was elected as the 32nd President of the United States, his "New Deal" policy was to provide an enormous measure of hope and inspiration for the people. Employment and relief became available through the many federal agencies that were organized to stabilize the recovery. On

January 22, 1932, Congress established the Reconstruction Finance Corporation (RFC) to make federal loans to banks in an effort to stimulate business.

Congress passed the National Industrial Recovery Act, commonly known as the NRA on June 16, 1933. The Civilian Conservation Corps (CCC) was established as a government agency to recruit the unemployed youth for service on public works. The Federal Relief program began in May and prohibition ended on December 5, 1933 when President Roosevelt repealed the 18th (Prohibition) Amendment. On May 6, 1935, the Works Progress Administration (WPA) was established. It was to provide work for the unemployed. To take them off the list that provided relief and allowed the people to have their dignity back.

Tampa Red's (Hudson Whittaker) "It's Tight Like That" was among the highest sold of all blues record ever recorded going into the decade of the 1930s. It became so popular that Red had to re-record it to keep up with the demands while other artists were making cover records of the tune composed by Tampa's partner "Georgia Tom" Dorsey. Together, Tampa Red and "Georgia Tom recorded other hits that include, "Let's Get Drunk and Truck," and "Let Me Feel It." Dorsey, however, was motivated to put his music talents to the music he loved best, the gospels, thereby leaving the blues behind him. Tampa Red in the meantime decided to do something different. He formed a new group that he called his Chicago Five, (guitar, piano, string bass, clarinet, and trumpet). It was Red's augmented trio that paved the way for other larger groups. Chicago was the blues capitol and Tampa re-recorded his previous hit with "Georgia Tom, "Let Me Play with Your Poodle" with his Chicago Five. It became a new style of urban blues.

Following the tradition of the larger band,, other artists did likewise. Harlem Hamfats recorded "Oh Red" with his seven-piece band from Chicago. Urban blues singer 'Big Bill' Broonzy joined Chris Barber Jazz Band in Britain. Tampa Red was a quiet and friendly sort of a person who was always ready to give a helping hand to anyone who was in need of it. Red was very popular with the blues singers and musicians, so much so, that they all came to him for advise on what to record and how they could improve their style. In Chicago, Tampa had a big house. It contained a big rehearsal room and two other rooms set up as recording studios. Many groups that came from out of town would end up in Red's house to practice. They would ask Red for suggestions about the bands style or arrangements, and with some of Tampa's input they would go into the studio room and record a couple of tunes. He had the respect and confidence from his peers.

'Big Bill' Broonzy, another big favorite in Chicago along with his closest friend Tampa, talks about going fishing with Red in his autobiography. Arthur 'Big Boy' Crudup, a singer and guitarist from Mississippi credits his success to Tampa Red. While Arthur was singing on a street corner in Chicago, an agent from Bluebird Records approached Crudup and offered to record him on the RCA Victor's 'race' label, but he would only record him if he had original songs which Arthur did not have since Arthur would admit that he was not a songwriter. Arthur only sang someone else's tunes. He was excited however, about the possibility of making a record on a major label, yet, he was unhappy because he didn't have any original material. Crudup went to see Tampa and told him about his dilemma. Red took Arthur into one of his studios and helped him write a couple of songs. The songs were submitted to the agent from Bluebird and on September 6, 1946, Arthur recorded one of the biggest selling records, "That's All Right," thanks to Tampa Red.

'Big Bill' Broonzy from Scott, Mississippi played fiddle and guitar and played them well. In 1920, he settled down in Chicago and made several recordings. Following the tradition of his friend Tampa Red, he augmented his band by adding a trumpet, and clarinet, and called it his Memphis Five. Broonzy used this group for his nightclub appearances and record sessions. Like Tampa Red, Big Bill was a friendly and likeable person always ready to help. Often times he would record with other groups to give them support and help the sales of their records. He recorded with "Cripple" Clarence Lofton on "Brown Skin Girls."

Robert Brown (Washboard Sam), Broonzy's half brother asked Big Bill to join him on a session using additional instruments including Arnett Nelson on clarinet or Buster Bennett on alto saxophone along with Horace Malcolm on piano. The session proved to be a big hit for Washboard Sam. There were, "Washboard's Barrel House Song" and "Down at the Village Store" on the Bluebird label. Broonzy also joined William Gillum (Jazz Gillum) as he was know in the 1936 Bluebird hit, "Sarah Jane" with Jazz Gillum playing the harmonica as the leading instrument on the session.

John Lee 'Sonny Boy' Williamson was born in Jackson, Tennessee in 1916. He learned to play the harmonica at an early age and began traveling throughout the south playing on street corners and in small black clubs. In the decade of the '30s he settled down in Chicago and began playing with the top blues singers and musicians. He was invited to join them on record sessions. 'Sonny Boy' Williamson was the best harmonica player in the Chicago area.

Williamson made a complete change in the structure of the blues. It was his influence that brought the harmonica as the predominant front-line instrument. 'Big Bill' Broonzy used him on record dates and in his nightclub act. 'Sonny Boy' also worked with 'Sleepy' John Estes and with guitarist Robert Lee McCoy and 'Big' Bill Joe Williams and mandolin player Willie Hatcher. In 1937 he made his first record for Bluebird, "Good Morning School Girl." The success of this record brought on more sessions. There was, "Bad Luck Blues," "War Time Blues," "Sloppy Drunk Blues," :Big Apple Blues" and "mellow Chick Swing" with Broonzy, Willie Lacey and Blind John Davis on the session.

'Sonny Boy' Williamson was a pleasant, friendly person who always managed to find time to teach the young kids how to play the harmonica. He was especially well liked by the musicians he worked with. His biggest weakness they say was his heavy drinking. At times he would get into arguments or battle with the customers in the clubs where he would be performing. As could be expected, the inevitable happened. On June 1, 1948 he was stabbed in the head with an ice pick. He was found dead on his doorstep by his wife Lacey Belle. He was 32 years old.

In Chicago, the lyrics of the urban blues revealed aggressive, hard living conditions that were brought on by the Depression. Tampa Red, Big Bill Broonzy, Washboard Sam, John Lee 'Sonny Boy' Williamson and 'Jazz' Gillum were the backbone of this blues tradition that began at the beginning of the 1930s. However, towards the end of that decade, and in contrast to the urban blues, singers from Mississippi developed and introduced the 'Down Home' style of blues with a more positive attitude. Especially with the new federal programs that were organized under Roosevelt's "new Deal" policy. Charley Patton, 'Son' House, Robert Petway, Bukka White, Tommy McClennan and most influential of them all was Robert Johnson that provided this new approach to the blues.

Robert Johnson wanted more than anything else to be a good guitar player and a 'down home' blues singer. He was both. Johnson was given personal attention by two of his idols, 'Son' House and Willie Brown. 'Son' House was among the best of the delta bluesmen and had a major impact on the development of young musicians, including Robert Johnson and Muddy Waters. Johnson was also influenced by listening to the records of Leroy Carr, Lonnie Johnson (no relation), Kokomo Arnold and Skip James. Robert took his music lessons seriously and after one year of constant practicing, he developed a guitar playing style that was far more superior to those of his instructors. On his Columbia/Legacy Label album release recorded in 1936-37 titled "The Complete Recordings," Robert was labeled "King of the Delta Blues Singers," and later followed with "King of the Blues."

On his 1936 record, "Come on in my Kitchen," Robert played and sang the song with so much feeling and expression that in the audience wherever he performed men and women were seen crying over the sentimentality of the lyrics. Very often Robert would cry while singing the blues. Writing in the album's liner notes, Eric Clapton stated, "Robert Johnson to me is the most important blues musician who ever lived. He was absolutely true to his own vision and as deep as I have gotten into his music over the last thirty years, I have never found anything more deeply soulful than Robert Johnson. His music remains the most powerful cry that I think you can find in the human voice, really."

    Keith Richards of the Rolling Stones also wrote in the same liner notes, "To me, Robert Johnson's influence---he was like a comet or a meteor that came along and, BOOM, suddenly he raised the ante, suddenly you just had to aim that much higher." However, there was another side of Robert Johnson. The views some people had of him was that he was a drunk, a womanizer and often moody. Robert always had a passion for women. It made no difference if she was married or not. As he traveled from town to town he would also go from woman to woman. A line in his lyrics of "From Four Till Late," reads "A woman is like a dresser---some man's always ramblin' through its drawers."

    Legend has it that when Robert Johnson at his early stages of guitar playing was ridiculed by older guitarists as Charley Patton, 'Son' House and Willie Brown. Embarrassed, he disappeared for over a year and the story goes that he made a deal with the devil. He would give up his soul to the devil if only he could master the guitar. The intersection of U.S. Highway 61 and U.S. Highway 49 was the crossroads where he was supposed to have made his deal with the devil at mid-night. Many of Johnson's lyrics have demonic overtones. Songs like, "Me and the Devil Blues," in which he vows to "Beat my Woman until I Get Satisfied."

    When he was only 26 years old, Robert Johnson's life was cut short on August 16, 1938, by a jealous husband who poisoned him for making a play for his wife while playing at a dance in Greenwood, Mississippi. Robert's music was emulated by such notables as Muddy Waters, Roosevelt Sykes, Big Joe Williams, 'Sonny Boy' Williamson, Robert Junior Lockwood, Howlin' Wolf and scores of rock musicians and the Rolling Stones. "My Blue Heaven was one of the most popular songs in Robert Johnson's repertoire.

6

STRING, JUG AND WASHBOARD BANDS

Charley Patton was one of the most important blues singers from Mississippi and was a strong influence to future singers. Charley would love to clown around while playing his guitar. At times he would put the guitar between his legs or behind his head, often lying on the floor as he was playing. He was referred to as the "Founder of the Delta Blues" by his peers

Patton never did like to be settled in one place for any length of time. He moved around a lot, especially in the Mississippi Delta area where his favorite stop was at Will

Dockery's plantation. There he was recognized for his ability to clown around and still play a good delta blues style guitar. He was also known for his heavy drinking, fighting and always had his eyes focused on the women standing by listening to his singing. Charley made several hit records. His most popular was "Mississippi Bo Weavil Blues." His "High Water Everywhere" record was inspired by the 1927 Mississippi flood. Other hits followed such as, "Running Wild Blues, A Spoonful Blues," "Pon Blues," and "High Sheriff Blues." In his "Moon Going Down" recording, he used rhythm guitar player Willie Brown to accompany him.

When Mississippi was experiencing a farming crisis in 1930, Charley Patton recorded "Dry Spell Blues." In his prime, Charley was a legend. His visible appearance in the Mississippi Delta area was an inspiration for other blues singers. Included were, Tommy Johnson, Willie Brown, 'Son' House, Chester Burnett (Howlin' Wolf), Bo Weavil Jackson, 'Crying' Sam Collins, J.D. 'Jelly Jaw' Short and his half brother Sam Chatmon.

Patton was not known to be a religious man, but in 1934 he recorded several sacred songs that he learned from Bill C. Patton, an Elder in his church and also married to Charley's mother. Bill raised Charley from childhood. One of the hymns that Charley recorded on Vocalion Records in New York was "On Death" and he used the pseudonym Elder J.J. Hadley. Bill C. Patton was not Charley's biological father. He was the result of one of his mother's earlier lovers. Henderson Chatmon, a fiddler and father of a musical family of a black string band that performed for a predominantly white audience during the 1920s and '30s. They called themselves the "Mississippi Sheiks."

Charley spent much of his youth with the Chatmon family and Sam Chatmon, son of Henderson referred to Patton as his half brother. The Mississippi Sheiks, eleven in number were versatile in their performance. Their instrumentation included the clarinet, piano, guitars and fiddles. The band's repertoire was a variety of music, blues, ragtime, jazz, spirituals, show tunes, minstrel tunes and white country dance music. They recorded over 50 sides for the Okeh Label. Some of their biggest hits were, "Loose Like That," "Sitting On Top of the World," "Stop and Listen Blues" and "Blood in My Eyes." These tunes were so successful in the 1930s that Howlin' Wolf, Hackberry Ramblers, Doc Watson, Bob Dylan, Ray Charles, Eric Clapton and the Grateful Dead made cover records on the same tunes.

It was Bo Carter (Armenter Chatmon), born on March 21, 1893 in Bolton, Mississippi that was the most popular of the Sheiks. Together with his brother Sam and a couple of other members of the band recorded "That Jazz Fiddler," "Sales Tax" and a remake with a smaller band of "Loose Like That." Charley Patton played with the Sheiks. Bo Carter made a successful career as a solo blues artist and made several records in the 1930s. Bo was exceptionally popular with the white audience and they would pay him well for his performances. On one of his tours in Memphis, Bo was stricken with a brain hemorrhage and became blind. On September 21, 1964 he died in poverty. He was 71 years old.

Mississippi has been known to be the land where the blues was born. The singers and guitarist coming from that area were establishing their regional styles and using whatever makeshift instruments available. Their music was labeled "Down Home Blues," "Country Blues" or "Rural Blues." Their blues were commonly called folk music. Paramount Records was quick to capitalize on this southern folk blues exposure and recorded 'Papa' Charlie Jackson's "Papa's Lawdy Lawdy Blues," in 1924 with a banjo background. With the success of this country blues Paramount recorded Blind Lemon Jefferson's "Long Lonesome Blues" with an authentic rural blues effect that was accepted by the black population.

'Papa' Charlie Jackson was born in New Orleans, Louisiana in 1885. At an early age he became fascinated with the sound of the banjo and taught himself how to play it well. Jackson was an easy going man, always cheerful and oftentimes witty and a very kind hearted person. In 1925 Paramount Records recorded another one of his hits, "Shave 'Em Dry." Jackson's records were sold throughout the entire country and people were playing his records over and over just to hear his pleasant voice and the full sound of his six string banjo. His country blues hits were, "I'm Alabama Bound," "Salty Dog," "Spoonful" and "Shake That Thing." At the age of 50, Papa Charlie Jackson died in Chicago in 1935.

In the decade of the 1920s, record companies were directing their attention to the Mississippi Delta and Memphis for their upcoming recording artists. They were primarily looking for singers who could accompany themselves with the guitar. A few were successful, but by the mid-1920s, the companies soon learned that the blues whether it be 'country blues', 'rural blues', 'down home blues' or 'dirty blues' was not intended to be a 'one man' show.

Jug bands provided the novelty acts for the medicine shows and rural picnics. A jug band usually consisted of a jug that someone would blow across the top opening to make it sound like a bass instrument, strings, a melody instrument that could be a clarinet, harmonica or kazoo and sometimes a guitar or banjo. Very often a washboard would be used to provide the rhythm with the player using a thimble, a nail, a fork or any metal object to scrape across the corrugated metal washboard.

The Dixieland Jug Blowers from Louisville, Kentucky recorded "Skip Skat Doodle Do" and "Southern Shout" for Victor Records in 1926, one of the earliest jug bands ever to record. Clifford Hayes, its leader and violinist included a trombone, alto saxophone and was successful to engage Earl'Fatha' Hines to play piano on this Victor recording of "Banjoreno," Hayes used three banjos for this minstrel song. Louisville was the place where the jug bands got started.

Gus Cannon's Jug Stompers with Ashley Thompson and Noah Lewis were considered the best of all jug bands in the 1920s.

Gus was born and raised on a plantation in Mississippi made a banjo from a frying pan and recorded his first record, "Can You Blame The Coloured Man?" using the name Banjo Joe on the label in 1927. The following year in 1928, he recorded "Heart Breakin' Blues, "Feather Bed," "Mingle wood Blues and "Viola Lee Blues" with the Cannon Jug Stompers on the Victor Label. Theses sides were later revived by the Grateful Dead. Gus Cannon's fame did not last very long. The last 40 years of his life he was pushing a broom in the streets in Memphis for a living.

Other jug bands to follow were Will Shade's Memphis Jug Band. Jack Kelly's South Memphis Jug Band had a successful hit with "Highway No.61 Blues" for Melotone Records. The Alabama based Birmingham Jug Band recorded "Getting Ready for Trial" on Okeh Records. Guitarist Bob Coleman's Cincinnati Jug Band did a fine recording of "Newport Blues" for the Paramount Label, and Walter Taylor and the Washboard Trio recorded "Diamond Ring" for Gennett Records in 1930.

Will Shade and his Memphis Jug Band played a prominent role along with Gus Cannon, Jack Kelly and Charlie Burse in keeping the jug bands active in the southern cities during the 1920s and 1930s. Jug bands were constantly called upon to perform in clubs, picnics, dances, political rallies, birthday parties, stag parties, and store openings, civic events in public parks, on riverboats, medicine shows and on trains. Their library included blues, ragtime music, minstrel songs, jazz and various types of dance music. Their audiences consisted of both blacks and whites.

The Memphis Jug Band recorded about 100 songs from 1927 to 1934. Very often they would record under different names. In 1932, they used the name Picaninny Jug Band. Memphis Minnie McCoy recorded two sides in 1930 with the members of the Picaninny Jug Band, but they used the pseudonym of Jed Davenport and his Beale Street Jug Band, Will Shade continued to bring talented performers into his band and most of them ventured out to be leaders of their own band. One of them was Charlie Burse, a highly talented guitar player, singer and dancer, inspired young Elvis Presley with his pelvic gyrations in the early 1950s. Alcohol claimed Will Shade's death in 1966.

The Alabama based Birmingham Jug Band recorded an extremely fine version of "Getting Ready for Trial," on the Okeh Label in 1930. Guitarist Bob Coleman's Cincinnati Jug Band made a hit for Paramount Records with their "Newport Blues." In 1935 Clifford Hayes and his Black Louisville Jug Band recorded a big seller for Bluebird Records with "My Good Gal's Gone Blues." In 1933 a New York white group called Rooftop Singers recorded Gus Cannon's 1928 hit "Walk Right In." The cover version was an immediate success that started a revival of college jug bands.

The Washboard Band was closely related to the jug band. It had a washboard that could be used as a rhythm instrument. String instruments like a guitar, banjo, or a one-string bass, a kazoo, harmonica or comb covered with a thin tissue paper. Washboard bands are mainly used as novelty bands. Blues singers often used them for accompaniment in record sessions. Women singers, Jennie Clayton, Hattie Hart and Laura Dukes particularly like using the washboard bands. Washboard Sam (Robert Brown) enjoyed his hits of "Rack 'Em' Back" and "Levee Camp Blues" for Bluebird Records. He played the washboard while singing. Occasionally, washboard bands would use wind instruments on their record sessions. The Washboard Rhythm Kings and the Washboard Serenaders used 2 trumpets and 3 saxophones on their records. Towards the end of the 1930s, the novelty of the washboard band faded away and they returned to their usual folk blues.

String bands were common throughout the south. Their instrumentations are guitars, mandolins, and string bass. The Mississippi Sheiks as mentioned earlier was by far the most popular of all string bands. Coley Jones' Dallas String Band was fortunate to record "Dallas Rag" and "Shine" for Columbia Records. For some unknown reason, string bands did not appeal to record companies. Sid Hemphill had an excellent band but was not lucky enough to get a label to record. Columbia however, was satisfied with the success of the Dallas String Band's version of "Rolling Mill Blues," "900 Miles" and the "Skin Game Blues." On another 'Peg Leg' session they recorded the country-dances of "Beaver Slide Rag" and "Peg Leg Stomp."

In the 1930s white string bands were recording the blues. Among them were the Leake County Revelers and the Carolina Tar Heels. Following the success of his "Long Lonesome Blues," Blind Lemon Jefferson born in Couchman, Texas in 1897 was the most influential folk blues singer that other singers were emulating. He lost his sight in early childhood and began singing in the streets throughout Texas. He was a wanderer. Would not settle down in one place long enough to call home.

In the three years that he remained as Paramount Records leading artist, Jefferson recorded many hits. Among them were, "Match Box Blues," "Pneumonia Blues," "Blind Lemon's Penitentiary Blues," "Hangman's Blues" and "One Dime Blues. His fame and popularity branched out to the south and mid-western states of Oklahoma, Mississippi, Louisiana, Alabama and Texas. Blind Lemon liked to work in house parties where he made a good deal of money. Victoria Spivey was a constant companion and would travel all over with him. Her primary responsibility was to take care of his money. Most of the house parties were arranged by pimps who would bring their women in and everyone attending had a good time, including Jefferson. Tips were generous, especially after a guest would request a song that he sings. His lyrics depicted that of 'wild women', 'heavy-hip mamas', 'bad liquor', 'sex' and dirty mistreaters'.

Many singers and musicians had comments to be made about Blind Lemon Jefferson. He would "take sympathy with the fellow" said St. Louis singer Henry Townsend. Roscoe Holcomb, a white musician from Kentucky said, "Up till then the blues were only inside me; Blind Lemon was the first to 'let out' the blues." "What I liked about Lemon's music most was that he made a clear chord," said Delta Bluesman Howlin' Wolf. Jefferson often had other singers and musicians traveling with him or just hanging around to be in his presence. Victoria Spivey, Lead belly, T-Bone Walker and Sam Chatmon were among them.

Blind Lemon had become the "King" of country blues. Paramount Records were so proud of his many hits that they designed a special lemon-colored label for his records only. At the young age of 33 at the height of his success, Jefferson was poisoned by a jilted jealous woman in Chicago in 1930.

Huddie William Ledbetter (Leadbelly) was born on January 29, 1885 in Mooringsport, Louisiana. His uncle bought him an accordion when he was five years old. Leadbelly also taught himself how to play the guitar and when he was 21 years old he left home to travel and play his guitar. Because of his brashness, he found himself more in jail than out. In 1916, he was in a Texas jail for assault charges, but managed to escape and changed his name to Walter Boyd. Two years later he killed a man in a fight and was charged with murder. After seven years of hard labor in a Texas' State Prison Farm, he begged the Governor for a pardon by composing a song that got his release. In 1930, he was arrested again for attempt homicide.

Under the guidance of John Lomax and his son Alan, who were representatives for the Library of Congress looking for a collection of work-songs, ballads, folk-songs and spirituals for recordings.In their search, they (John and Alan) found that Leadbelly was their best discovery. John Lomax petitioned the Governor for Leadbelly's release and it was granted. Leadbelly's most popular song was "Goodnight Irene." He traveled throughout the United States and Europe where he fell ill and died of lateral sclerosis on December 6, 1949.

7

FIELD RECORDINGS

Nothing could have been more influential on the development of the blues than the field recordings. Record companies in the early 1920s dispatched talent scouts into the Deep South to search out potential blues artists of the future.

Record companies were encouraging the blacks to sing their original songs for the sole purpose of enhancing this new music to attract the younger people. In addition to promoting the blues as a new music, the record companies retained the copyrights of the blues and secured the royalties from them. Not all field recordings were of the blues type. The blacks sang ballads, spirituals, gospels, work-songs, protest-songs, barrel-house songs and the blues. Also, not all of the field recordings were made by songsters. Some recordings were made with string bands, brass bands, washboard bands and jug bands.

Field recordings were made on location with non-professionals as well as with professionals that traveled with the medicine shows, vaudeville circuit, carnivals and minstrel shows. As can be expected, these field recordings had successfully enhanced the careers of rural and classic blues singers. The unsung heroes of these discoveries were the talent scouts who with a keen ear for music recognized the talents of the artists and recorded them. Lawrence Gellert of Greenville, South Carolina was among the first to make a field recording in 1924. He was followed by other notable scouts such as, Frank Walker in New York, Arthur Laibley in Chicago, Polk Brockman from Atlanta, Georgia and H.C. Speir in Jackson, Mississippi.

Field recordings gave a clearer description of the mood and feelings of the blacks as they were singing what they were enduring. Gellert would search out his discoveries in the chain-gangs where the singers would chant about protest and hardships of their mistreatments by the white guards. "Down in the Chain-Gang" was recorded by an unknown singer on Heritage Label in 1924 by Gellert with the lyrics describing the singer's dilemma.

Robert W. Gordon, the first field recording administrator for the Library of Congress recorded "Glory to God My Son's Come Home" in 1926. Gordon's recording interest was the work songs, ragtime, spirituals and gospels and had very little regard for the blues. In 1933, he was removed from his position and replaced by John A. Lomax as curator. John, along with his son Alan traveled the southern states and made numerous blues recordings. His first stop was at the Louisiana State Penitentiary at Angola. Huddie Ledbetter, A.K.A. Ledbetter provided a number of songs for Lomax to record. With his 12 string guitar, Leadbelly sang some ballads, like, "Ella Speed." "Becky Deem, She Was A Gamblin' Gal" and "Frankie and Albert" which was later changed to "Frankie and Johnny." Leadbelly boasted that he was the "King of the twelve-string guitar player of the world." He recorded his biggest hit "Good Morning Blues" for the Bluebird Label in 1940.

After leaving Angola, John and Alan Lomax traveled to other prisons in the south for more talent. Pete Harris was discovered in Richmond, Virginia. He was the second important black singer and guitarist for John Lomax. Harris sang his songs in the same fashion as Blind Lemon Jefferson. His songs included, "Jack and Betsy," "Blind Lemon's Song" and "Alabama Bound." Things could not have gone any better for John and Alan Lomax. Everywhere they went with the field recording equipment in the back seat of their car, they were successful in finding good talent.

In Florida, harmonica player Booker T. Sapps recorded "Alabama Blues." At the state farm in Lynn, Virginia, singer Jimmie Strothers recorded the blues "Goin' to Richmond." Guitarist Gabriel Brown recorded "Education Blues" in Eatonville, Florida. At the Clemens State Farm in Brazonia, Texas guitarist Smith Casey recorded a beautiful ballad called "Shorty George."

Blind Willie McTell was recorded in Atlanta, Georgia. Bukka White's recordings were from the Parchman Farm State Penitentiary in Mississippi and Oscar 'Buddy' Woods in Shreveport, Louisiana. John Lomax received great reviews about Leadbelly's recordings that he returned to the Louisiana State Penitentiary to make more records of Leadbelly. On this second visit they recorded "Baby, Low Down, Oh Low down Dirty Dog," a scintillating blues. Lomax knew that he had one of the best blues singers in Leadbelly, but he wasn't much good to him while he was in prison. So, Lomax suggested that Leadbelly compose a pardon song that he could present to Governor O.K. Allen of

Louisiana to set Leadbelly free.Leadbelly chose the popular song "Irene" for his apologetic lyrics for his pardon.

Keeping his promise, Lomax took the record to the Governor and with a little persuasion got Leadbelly's pardon. In appreciation for John's efforts to get his release from prison Huddie offered to drive Lomax's car to other field locations. After several months had passed, Leadbelly and John went separate ways leaving Leadbelly to establish himself to the public as a guitarist-singer available for work. John Lomax continued on with his field recordings and to places like the State Penitentiary at Huntsville, Texas, the Cumins State Farm in Gould, the Central State Farm at Sugarland, Texas and the Bellwood Prison Camps in Georgia. Also on his itinerary were lumber camps, plantations, barrelhouse joints and loading docks.

The field recordings were instrumental in discovering such notables as, "Ivory Joe" Hunter, Henry Trevellian, Blind Jesse Harris, Albert Ammons, Meade "Lux" Lewis, Jimmie Johnson, Sonny Terry, Blind Boy Fuller, 'Son' House, Willie Brown, McKinley Morganfield (Muddy Waters), Willie Blackwell and others. The end of the first phase of field recordings that started in 1924 was in the 1940s. The recordings included ballads, work-songs, folk-songs, gospels, spirituals, plantation songs, field hollers and the blues.

The second phase of field recordings was from 1946 to 1960. With the upgraded recording equipment, much of the earlier recordings were re-recorded with clearer fidelity. William Russell, owner of American Music Records took to the road with a more sophisticated recording system and recorded "Stomp de Lowdown" and "Drink's Blues" by Ollie 'Dink' Johnson in 1946. Alan Lomax recorded work-songs, ballads and blues from inmates at the Mississippi State Penitentiary in Parchman in 1947. Frederic Ramsey Jr. arrived in New York in 1948 to record all of Leadbelly's collection of songs. One of the songs that Huddie composed was of a protest nature, "Nobody in the World is better than Us."

Pete Seeger and John Lomax Jr. recorded black inmates at the Ramsey State Farm in Otey, Texas in 1951. The Ramsey Prison band consisting of trombone, two saxophones, piano, bass and drums recorded their popular blues, "Lowdown Dirty Shame." Bluesman James Lowry recorded "Tampa Blues" in 1953. Billie Pierce and her trumpet playing husband recorded "Careless Love" in 1954. Blind Willie McTell recorded "Salty Dog" in 1956. Reverend Blind Gary Davis recorded "Candy Man" and Hesitation Blues, in 1957. Pianist Speckled Red, James Cruthfield and James Robinson were recorded in 1957 by talent scout Erwin Helfer "Baby Please Don't Go, by Joe Williams for talent scout Robert Koester in 1958.

Scrapper Blackwell, Leroy Carr's former guitarist was back in the recording studio in 1958. When Carr died of alcoholism in 1935, Scrapper could never get over the shock of his partner's death and dropped out of the music scene until 1958 when he was re-discovered in Indianapolis. The session produced "Little Girl Blues," "Little Boy Blues" and an instrumental of "Cherry." 1960 saw the end of the second phase of field recordings. During this period, the spotlight was on the talents of Snooks Eaglin, K.C. Douglas, Sam 'Lightnin' Hopkins, Willie B. Thomas, Robert Pete Williamson, John Jackson, Mance Lipscomb, Robert Johnson, Champion Jack Dupree and others.

8

EXODUS TO NORTHERN CITIES

Memphis, Tennessee is the home of America's greatest music-the blues. Beale Street was the corner of black commerce and entertainment where the clubs and bars featured some of the best in the world. There were Hammitt Ashford's saloon at the corner of Beale and 4th Streets, which was the oldest bar in Memphis that catered to the middle and upper class of people. The Monarch Saloon was strictly a black bar where white would neither be served nor welcomed.

W.C. Handy had his band playing in "Pee Wee's Saloon" frequented by professional gamblers, jockeys, racetrack men and members of the Memphis mob. Howard Yancy's pool hall was a hangout for musicians with an upstairs room for groups to practice. The Palace Theater on Beale and Hernando featured Alberta Hunter who confessed to being a lesbian and had often picked-up prostitutes in the streets for her sexual gratification. Beale Street was a haven for cheap stores, eating places, juke joints and a popular whorehouse. Cocaine was sold by the merchants openly in as little as ten cent portions. The Lorraine Motel just off of Beale Street was also a place of business for dope dealers and prostitutes.

Schwab's Dry Goods Store on Beale Street offered saleable items as blues records, grain, chewing tobacco, overalls and drugs. The Orpheum Theater was located at the far end of Beale Street by the river. Women entertainers, especially those with cocaine and whiskey habits, would encourage men wherever they are performing that they were most welcomed to Beale Street. One of the three most popular women was Alberta Hunter who not only attracted men but women as well. Memphis Minnie McCoy was kept busy with the men with a two dollar a trick price tag. Lil Hardin, Louis Armstrong's wife was also a favorite with the men. Beale Street was the home of the Theater Owners Booking Association (T.O.B.A.), sometimes known as "Toby-Time" and often referred to by black entertainers as "tough on black asses."

Walter 'Furry' Lewis was a regular performer on Beale Street and would play with W.C. Handy's band whenever they were in town. Aleck 'Rice' Miller, 'Sonny Boy' Williamson was the leader of the house band for the "King Biscuit Time" radio show on station KFFA in Memphis. His personnel included Robert Junior Lockwood on guitar, James 'Peck' Curtis on drums, pianist Joe 'Pine Top' Perkins and 'Sonny Boy' playing the harmonica.

The jug bands found a home in Memphis and especially on Beale Street where they would perform at clubs, juke joints, picnics, on the street corners, in the city parks, and other ventures. Musicians that were associated with jug bands were Allen Shaw, Little Boy Doyle, Kaiser Clifton and James DeBerry and much more. Memphis however, was a stop-over for musicians traveling north from the Deep South. When the "Jazz Age" began in 1920, blacks had already begun their exodus from the south to what they considered to be their "Promise Land" up north. Any place was better than the south for the Negro. The black population grew up in cities like Chicago, Detroit, Washington, D.C., Philadelphia, Newark and New York. They brought with them the music of the classic blues singers, the country blues, rural blues and the down home blues.

Northern white singers and musicians were picking up on the authentic black blues music. As a matter of fact, it was Blind Lemon Jefferson who had the most influence with the white man's blues. More and more northern nightclubs and cabarets were hearing the true blues as performed by the black artists.

Arthur Blake (Blind Blake) was born in Jacksonville, Florida in 1895. He was an accomplished singer and guitarist and was well known and very popular in Florida, Georgia, Tennessee, Detroit and several other eastern states. Paramount Records recorded about 80 sides with Blind Blake between the years 1926 to 1932. Being an excellent musician, some of his sides were strictly instrumental. His unequaled guitar playing was demonstrated on his "Blind Arthur's Breakdown," "He's in the Jailhouse Now," and "Come On Boys Let's Do that Messin' Around." His singing was pleasant with a melancholy sound that can be heard on "Cold Hearted Mama Blues" and "Search Warrant Blues." He often teamed up with pianist Charlie Spand. At the age of 40, Blind Blake died in 1935.

'Race' records were selling as fast as the record companies could get them out in the market place. 1927 through 1930 were the boom years. All forms of black music were selling especially blues and gospels. The search for new talent was on by the five major companies, Columbia, Paramount, Vocalion, Bennett and Victor. They had talent scouts on the road looking for and recording any new singer or group. One of the main scouts was Thomas Andrew Dorsey, born in Villa Rica, Georgia in 1899. He got his music education at the Chicago College of Composition and Arranging. He was certainly qualified to recognize good talent when he heard it, being an excellent pianist and blues singer himself. Under his professional name, "Georgia Tom," he made several recordings with the "Mother of the Blues," 'Ma Rainey, and featuring 'Tampa Red' (Hudson Whittaker) on guitar. In 1928 the duo of Dorsey and Tampa Red recorded their blues hit "Tight Like That" and followed it with "Terrible Operation Blues." In 1930, he left the blues and formed his Gospel Songs Music Publishing Company and by 1931 he was promoting gospel music exclusively.

Discovered during this wide spread talent search was Blind Willie McTell from Statesboro, Georgia who played a twelve-string guitar and was constantly heard singing on street corners in his hometown and in Atlanta. He was versatile in his music. He was equally at ease whether playing slow blues, minstrel show songs, ragtime music, gospels, spirituals or hillbilly music. His big hit was "Statesboro Blues." He died in 1959 at the age of 58 in Atlanta, Georgia.

'Peg Leg' Howell and his Gang with Henry Williams on guitar and Eddie Anthony playing fiddle was heard as they were playing on the corner of Decatur Street in Atlanta by Columbia Records representative Wilbur C. Brown who signed 'Peg Leg' to record four sides in 1926. Robert and Charlie Hicks, professionally known as Barbecue Bob and Charley Lincoln landed on the Columbia Label and recorded their first hit "Barbecue Blues." Their career was short-lived when Barbecue Bob died in 1931 of pneumonia and Charley took to heavy drinking.

As the 1920s ended, the nation entered into the 1930s with great economic Depression that began on October 29, 1929 with the stock market crash. The stock losses from 1929 to 1931 were estimated at fifty billion dollars. 2300 banks were forced to close. The Depression also took its toll on the music industry. Record companies were cutting back on their pressings. Singers and musicians were not working along with the rest of the nation. Whatever little money they had was soon disappearing. The

Depression affected everyone. Blacks, whites, southerners, northerners, the rich, the poor, it made no difference.

Conditions were so bad that blues musicians and singers had to revert to the 'chitlin circuit' where they would play at house-rent parties to raise money to pay the rent that was currently due plus money to pay other outstanding bills and for food. At these parties the guest would pay an admission fee of twenty-five cents or whatever they could afford. Some guests that were a little more solvent than others would contribute as mush as fifty-cents. For their donations they would be served a good portion of chitlins, tastily seasoned with salt, pepper, celery, cubed potatoes and Tabasco with some black-eyed peas as a side dish.

House-rent parties were springing up all over the country in the poorer neighborhoods. Performers would play at several different houses within the community, and at each of these parties chitlin was served. It was a very cheap meal to prepare. The Depression was to last throughout the four year presidency of Herbert Hoover. It was the worst financial gloom ever experienced not only in the United States but in Europe also.

Georgia Tom played at rent parties in Chicago and said that he would play for three or four and only got thirty-five cents a night. A couple of times (not often) he got as much as fifty-cents. Some pianist like Speckled Red and a few others were more fortunate. They were playing their music in homes and apartments sponsored by the pimps who provided prostitutes, gambling, liquor, food and political protection, where all it took was money for the police not to know or see anything. As far as the police were concerned, they saw nothing illegal going on. It was just a common way of life.

Speckled Red stated that "dancing was the life of the party." After a few drinks, they were tap dancing or doing the black bottom or the buck and wing, while others were doing a "hands on" dance that is their hands were all over each other's body.

Pianist Romeo Nelson, while playing at one of these exclusive house parties in Chicago, was asked to play his hit record of "Getting' Dirty Just Shakin' That Thing." It was a time and place where anything goes. People got so drunk that they were performing sexual acts on the floor, on the couch, against the wall in plain view for all to see. The people we're talking about at these parties are the "so-called" high-class society group, who, when they are sober would look down their noses at the low class (as they would call them) singers and musicians.

During the 1920s the prime time of the classic blues singers, the guitar was the main instrument associated with the blues. There were however, several blues pianist from the south. Some of them were capable of playing both instruments. Skip James played the piano and guitar equally well as demonstrated on the Paramount hit record of "Little Cow and Calf is Gonna Die Blues." In the late 1920s and into the early 1930s, southern blues piano players were moving out of the south and into the northern cities where the action was taking place. There was always a piano in brothels, and saloons often referred to as barrelhouses, where the clientele would invariably be the hard drinking lumberjacks and shipyard workers. The piano player would be entertaining the group while playing the blues. Hardly a night would go by without a fight among the patrons who couldn't hold their liquor. Because of this frequent occurrence, the piano blues style came to be labeled as barrelhouse music. Some of the pianist working in barrelhouses were, Speckled Red, Roosevelt Sykes, Memphis Slim, Champion Jack Dupree and Eurreal 'Little Brother' Montgomery. Barrelhouse music was the product of the black American blues musicians.

Barrelhouses blues was played with a left-hand vamp played very heavy or 'stomping' which always required four steady beats to a bar. (See Example 1).

EXAMPLE 1

Occasionally, a 'walking bass' in 4/4 meter would be employed in the barrelhouse blues. (See Example 2)

example 2

Texas pianist Will Ezell's "Barrel House Man," "The Dirty Dozen" by Speckled Red and Charlie Spann's "Soon This Morning" are excellent examples of barrelhouse music, and probably the most influential of all barrelhouse music was Charles

'Cow Cow' Davenport's "Cow Cow Blues" with his heavy left hand walking bass.

Meade 'Lux' Lewis was among the first to introduce the fast piano playing blues to be called 'boogie-woogie' along with new urban blues that were growing in popularity. Although boogie-woogie was played in the same brothels and beer joints with barrelhouse blues, there was a noticeable difference in their styles. Boogie-woogie music was primarily played for dancing with a faster tempo than barrelhouse. The left hand played the bass notes in regular octaves (See Example 3) or in broken octaves (See Example 4).

example 3

EXAMPLE 4

Although boogie-woogie was played in the early 1920s, "The Rocks" by Clay Cluster in 1923, Meade 'Lux' Lewis' "Honky Tonk Train Blues" and Charles 'Cow Cow' Davenport's "Cow Cow Blues" followed shortly afterwards. But it was Clarence 'Pine Top' Smith's biggest selling record in 1929 of "Pine Top's Boogie-woogie that started the influx of record sales in the 'race' record market. Romeo Nelson's "Head Rag Hop," "Indiana Avenue Stomp" by Arthur 'Montana' Taylor and Charles Avery's "Dearborn Street Breakdown" soon followed.

The piano style of boogie-woogie was slowly declining by the end of the 1930s. However, on December 23, 1938, Meade 'Lux' Lewis along with Albert Ammons and Pete Johnson, three distinct capable boogie-woogie pianists was part of a concert at Carnegie Hall, in New York City, called "From Spirituals to Swing," that gave new life to the piano style of boogie-woogie. The theme of the concert according to its promoter and organizer John Hammond was to trace the history of black American music from its beginnings in Africa to the present day. The performance was so successful that an encore concert was performed on Christmas Eve.

Author at Percy Mayfield's piano — Betty Miller

Lowell Fulson   Betty Miller   Lee King — Betty Miller

Tina Mayfield at her husband's piano — Betty Miller

Betty Miller's 'Blues' room — Betty Miller

B.B.KIng   Willie Dixon   John Lee Hooker   Betty Miller

Buddy Guy   Betty Miller

John Lee Hooker   Bonnie Raitt

'Big' Joe Turner

Billy Branch   Betty Miller

Solomon Burke   Betty Miller

Percy Mayfield   'Big' Joe Turner   Betty Miller

Blues, Then and Now/Leanza

Sunnyland Slim   Eddie Boyd   Memphis Slim

Betty Miller

Betty Miller's 'Blues' room   Betty Miller

Clarence 'Gatemouth' Brown   Betty Miller

Betty Miller's 'Blues' room Betty Miller

Blues, Then and Now/Leanza

Koko Taylor   B.B. King   Betty Miller

9

LEADBELLY AND MUDDY WATERS

Huddie Ledbetter, better known as Leadbelly. Why that nickname name? No one knows for sure. But what is certain is that he was the first country blues artist to be accepted by the white public. His variety of music included work songs, cowboy songs, blues, spirituals, songs about life in prison on which he had first hand experience, folk songs and the current ballads of the day. He has been singing and playing his twelve-string guitar on street corners and in bars throughout Dallas, Texas, since he was 15 years old.

Leadbelly was musically versatile being able to play in addition to his guitar, the piano, accordion and the harmonica as well. When he was 16 years old, he took off for Shreveport, Louisiana where he got a job playing piano in one of the main brothels in town. In his late teens, Huddie had a reputation as being a short tempered, heavy drinker, a womanizer and always in the center of any violence. In Dallas around 1950, he came in contact with Blind Lemon Jefferson in a saloon where Jefferson was performing. They became good friends and Leadbelly acted as his guide. But it was Huddie's nature to be in trouble. Trouble followed him every where he went. For a number of crimes, violence and assaults he put in many years on the chain gang, and in prisons in Texas and Louisiana.

In 1917, Leadbelly killed a man over a woman. For this he got 30 years of hard labor on a Texas prison farm. After serving only 8 years he was given a pardon by the Governor of Texas. His freedom didn't last long. In 1930, he was again sentenced to hard labor at the Angola State Penitentiary in Louisiana for assault with intent to kill a white man. He was pardoned a second time with the help of John A. Lomax, a recording representative for the Library of Congress. Leadbelly recorded "Match Box Blues," "If I Wasn't For Dicky," "Honey, I'm All Out and Down" and "Becky Deem, She was a Gamblin' Gal." On December 6, 1949, Leadbelly died of the Lou Gehrig's disease (Arterial Lateral Sclerosis) in New York. He was 64 years old.

During the mid-1940s, blues singers, Big Bill Broonzy, Lonnie Johnson, Roosevelt Sykes, Memphis Minnie, Tampa Red, Big Maceo and John Lee 'Sonny Boy' Williamson were very active singing in the black clubs in Chicago. Each had their own followers and was still recording with the 'race' record companies. Following close behind them were another group of young blues singers. Names like, Memphis Slim, Eddie Boyd, 'Baby Face Leroy' Foster, Sunnyland Slim and Robert Nighthawk who adopted the name from his 1937 record "Prowling Nighthawk."

It was however, Sunnyland Slim that introduced another young singer who was to be responsible for the transformation of Chicago blues. McKinley Morganfield was from the delta area in Rolling Fork, Mississippi was also known as Muddy Waters. The delta area is a 200 mile stretch of low, flat plains running between Memphis, Tennessee and Vicksburg, Mississippi, bordered by the

Mississippi River on the west and the Yazoo River on the east. He started his music career as a harmonica player and by the age of 17, he was playing the guitar. Muddy admits that he learned a good deal about guitar playing by listening repeatedly to Leroy Carr's 1928 record "How Long, How Long Blues" on which the famed guitarist Scrapper Blackwell was heard.

In the early 1940s, Muddy was found working as a field hand on Stovall's Farm in Clarksdale, Mississippi by Alan Lomax and had Waters make his first record for the Library of Congress, "I Be's Troubled" and "Country Blues." In 1943, he boarded the Illinois Central train to Chicago. When the train arrived at 12th and Michigan in the downtown section, just a few blocks from the south side black population and emptied the last three cars that were restricted for blacks only. It was remarked that it looked like 'the Ellis Island of the black migration."

As soon as Muddy Waters settled down to his own south side apartment, he immediately began working as a sideman with Memphis Slim, 'Sonny Boy' Williamson, Sunnyland Slim and most of the other top leading musicians. Word got around about his talent and he soon became in demand. Muddy was among the first to switch from the acoustic to the electric guitar. After teaming up with Big Bill Broonzy the leading blues artist along with his rival Tampa Red. Big Bill introduced Muddy to Lester Melrose, a white record producer who had an open door to RCA and Columbia Records. Melrose recorded Waters in 1946 and sold the masters to Columbia. Columbia executives however, decided not to release the sides because they were not acquainted with the sound of an electric guitar for the blues.

In 1947, Sunnyland Slim brought Muddy Waters to Aristocrat Records a new company that just settled in Chicago. Aristocrat owners, Leonard and Phil Chess took Muddy into the studio and recorded "Gypsy Woman" and "Little Anna May," both sides were financial flops for the Chess brothers. However, Waters with the assistance of Sunnyland Slim convinced the brothers to do one more session. Muddy worked out a duo with Big Crawford on string bass. The song was "I Can't Be Satisfied." The record became a local hit. The Chess brothers had records hand delivered to radio stations and it was heard throughout the immediate area. Muddy went on to make more records that became hits such as, "I'm Your Hoochie Coochie Man," "Rolling Stone," "Got My Mojo Workin'," and "I Just Want To Make Love To You." Waters became a worldwide superstar and were considered to be the best blues singer of all times.

By 1951, he had a list of tunes that were among the top ten R&B hits including "Honey Bee" and "Long Distance Call." When asked what contributed to his success, he would answer that he was a combination of three musicians, one part 'Son' House, one part Robert Johnson and one part Muddy Waters. He realized that there was more of an audience out there besides the blacks, and he began recording with white rock musicians. While he was in his prime, he helped several white musicians to get started. There were harmonica player Paul Butterfield and Paul Oscher who Muddy would use on his record dates.

Muddy's personal band that he took great pride in were with Little Walter (Jacobs) on harp, Otis Spann on piano, Fred Below on drums, Jimmy Rogers on Guitar and Willie Dixon playing bass. Waters was liked and respected as a bandleader because he gave each man a chance to show case his talent. Many blues singers at one time or another filtered through the Muddy Water's band. Names like, Big Walter Shakey Horton, Junior Wells, James Cotton, Buddy Guy, Earl Hooker, Paul Butterfield and Jimmy Rodgers. When Buddy Guy came into Chicago from his hometown in Louisiana in 1957, he was broke and hungry. Muddy heard him play guitar and sing and found work for Buddy and also got him a record date on Chess Records (formally Aristocrat).

In 1958, Muddy Waters and Otis Spann toured Europe and much to their surprise the European audiences were familiar with Muddy's hits. He continued to travel extensively throughout Europe and the United States. In 1970, Waters was involved in an automobile accident that confined him to a wheelchair. On April 30, 1983, Muddy Waters died in Chicago at the age of 68. Muddy's parting words were; "The blues had a baby, and they called it Rock and Roll."

10

HOWLIN' WOLF AND SONNY BOY WILLIAMSON II

While in Chicago and still in command as the top blues entertainer, Muddy Waters was constantly put on alert by the many drifters that came up north from the delta area to try and steal his thunder. One such drifter was a six-foot-six, 300 pound harmonica player who called himself Howlin' Wolf. His true name was Chester Burnett from West Point, Mississippi. As a youngster he worked on the plantation with his parents. By the time he was in his early teens he heard blues singer Charlie Patton and immediately fell in love with the music he was hearing.

Patton took Howlin' under his wing and taught him how to play the guitar. Howlin's father observed the interest and enthusiasm his son had for music that he bought him his first guitar at the age of 19. Wolf took to the road and was singing and playing his guitar throughout the south. It was in Arkansas where Howlin' met up with Alex 'Rice' Miller (Sonny Boy Williamson) as he called himself, and 'Rice' taught him how to play the harmonica. Wolf further advanced his music education when he came in contact with Tommy Johnson and Jimmy Rodgers, a white yodeler.

'Sonny Boy' Williamson married Howlin's half-sister, which brought a closer tie with his new brother-in-law. 'Sonny Boy' was touring the southern circuit with Robert Junior Lockwood, another blues singer and guitar player and they took Wolf along so that he may gain more experience in traveling on the road. Wolf was eager to learn. He observed every move 'Sonny Boy' and Lockwood made and he tried emulating them both. Howlin' even tried to copy Charley Patton's guitar solos, but he soon realized that he was not in the same ball park with any of them. So, Howlin' used his physical appearance to capture the attention of the audience.

His voice was loud and course with a growling effect. It was once remarked that when Howlin' whispers, you could hear him a block away. By nature Wolf gave the impression of being a mean and vengeful person taking advantage of his size to intimidate people. For instance, in 1969, there was a professional rivalry between Muddy Waters who was in full command of the Chicago area and the top record seller at the time, and Howlin' Wolf wanted that position. During the 1969 Ann Arbor Blues Festival, several of the top blues entertainers were invited to perform. Each artist was given an allotted time for their performance. Howlin' was also a favorite with the audience at the time. On the program, Wolf was to precede Muddy Waters who was to close the show. However, Howlin' Wolf had different plans. He deliberately stayed on stage long past his allotted time to prevent Waters from participating in the program. Yet, it was Muddy who helped Wolf get his first big job in Chicago in the early 1950s.

Howlin' Wolf made his first two-sided record while he was working on the plantation picking cotton. Leonard Chess, one of the owners of Chess Records traveled the delta area listening to the workers singing. When he heard Howlin', he hooked up his portable recorder and Wolf sang, "Saddle My Pony" and "Worried All the Time." As was the case with other artists, each had someone to look up to for guidance. Muddy Waters had 'Son' House, Elmore James was inspired by Robert Johnson and Howlin' Wolf followed after Charley Patton.

Wolf developed into a flamboyant performer. He would enter on stage crawling on his hands and knees in a wolf like fashion. He would hop and skip across the stage while singing and putting on all sorts of gyrations to entertain the audience. His act was so unusual that the Rolling Stones invited Wolf to appear on their American television show "Shindig" in 1964. That was Wolf's first experience with rock and roll.

Howlin' Wolf gained a lot of his experience by traveling and working with other artists. There were, Tommy McClennan, Mississippi Sheiks with Memphis Slim and Sam Chatmon, Charley Patton's half brother, 'Sonny Boy' Williamson, Jimmy Rodgers, Willie Dixon and others. While on the road, they often spent their time playing 'pitty pat' a popular card game among the blacks. Wolf went on to make records for Chess Records; "Moanin' at Midnight" was his first big hit. This was followed with other hits such as, "Spoonful," "Poor Boy," "Riding in the Moonlight," "The Red Rooster" and "Three Hundred pounds of Joy."

When Howlin' moved into Chicago, the first man to help him was Muddy Waters. Muddy got him bookings throughout the area that helped Wolf's popularity. Howlin' soon came to the realization that if he wanted to be king of Chicago's south side, he would have to outdo or topple Muddy Waters. Wolf however, was smart enough to know that he wasn't as good as an instrumentalist as the others, so, when he went in to record his sessions he employed the services of Ike Turner, Hubert Sumlin, Willie Johnson, Willie Dixon and others. His records were climbing on the R&B charts and his music became a means of inspiration for the British rock and rollers.

In 1971, Wolf suffered several heart attacks which limited his tours. Then in 1973 an automobile accident caused severe kidney injuries, this did not stop his performances however, even though they were limited and toned down he made his appearances. On January 10, 1976 he died in the Hines Veteran's Hospital. He was 66 years old.

Alex 'Rice' Miller (Sonny Boy Williamson) was a self taught musician. At the age of five, he was playing the harmonica and by the time he reached his tenth birthday he was touring the 200 mile stretch of the delta earning money to exist. Sonny Boy was born in 1897 in Mississippi. During the decades of the 1929 and 1930s he and his traveling musicians Robert Johnson and Arthur Crudup were playing in rural juke houses. Sonny Boy was among the best of the harmonica players. When he toured Europe with Crudup and Johnson they were on the same concert program with the popular British groups of Yardbird and the Animals.

In 19141, 'Rice' Miller was featured on the radio show "King Biscuit Time" on Station KTTA in Helena, Arkansas. It was during these radio broadcasts that Muddy Waters and B.B. King actually heard the sound of the authentic delta blues that eventually became the basis for the Chicago blues. Lillian McMurray, owner of Trumpet Records in Jackson, Mississippi heard 'Sonny Boy' and was emotionally impressed by his soulful playing and singing that she recorded a few sides with him in 1953 that became financial hits for her company.

'Sonny Boy' Williamson headed north to Chicago and began recording for Chess Records from 1955 and 1964 with much success. His heavy drinking and vulgar language got him into a lot of trouble often landing in jail for a short stay to cool off. During one of his heated arguments with the Chess brothers whom he disliked with a passion got so badly out of hand that it took Willie Dixon to calm down both parties. 'Rice' Miller took to the road again and headed back to Europe in the early 1960s. After a short visit he returned home in Helena and died in his sleep in 1965. He was 68 years old.

11

SOUL

      In the mid-1950s the public began hearing a change in the further development of the blues. It was the merging of blues and gospel music to form a new sound that became rhythm and blues. It was this marriage that would eventually evolve into soul music in the 1960s.

      Leading this trend was the Five Royales of North Carolina whose gospel rendition of "Baby Don't Do It" became a number one hit on Billboard's R&B charts on January 17, 1953. Ray Charles' career began in 1954 with his R&B version of "I Got a Woman." James Brown's 1956 hit of "Please, Please, Please," found its place on the R&B charts. During the early 1960s, soul music became the replacement for rhythm and blues. The pioneers of soul music were all black performers whose parents and some of the performers themselves have grown up during the Gospel Era. The term soul is closely associated with African-American cultures. Later, in the second half of 1969 when the music journal Billboard magazine officially replaced rhythm and blues to soul, that the scope of this music extended into the white population.

Preacher Solomon Burke from Philadelphia, Pennsylvania was among the first to record a hit with his soul version of "Just out Of Reach (Of My Two Open Arms)," on Atlantic Records in 1961. Burke followed through with two successive hits in 1962 and 1963. They were "Cry to Me," and "If You Need Me" respectively. Many blues singers and musicians included soul music in their repertoire. Among the most influential of them all was Bobby 'Blue' Bland whose national 1962 hit "Yield Not to Temptation" is an excellent example of what the combination of gospel and blues sound like.

Aretha Franklin, America's Queen of Soul's hit "I Never Loved a Man the Way I Love You" and "Chain of Fools" was a blend of gospel and blues. Aretha's input to music was unique in that she was labeled simultaneously as the "Queen of Soul" and the "Queen of the Blues." Yet her audiences categorized her as being of one type. B.B. King on the other hand popularized soul music to a new high with his guitar and vocal backed with a solid big band arrangement. King displayed his talent on "Let the Good Time Roll" and "Stormy Monday Blues."

Buddy Guy, Otis Rush and Magic Sam were three guitarists and singers from Chicago that took on the rhythm and blues sound along with gospel that associated them with soul. Buddy teamed up with Junior Wells traveling the Fillmore Circuit during the 1960s and 1970s to promote his hit album "Damn Right, I've Got the Blues" and "Feels like Rain" which were widely accepted by the white audiences. Otis Rush got his recognition with the success of his first record on the Cobra Label "I Can't Quit You Baby" and

"Jump Sister Bessie." "All Your Love" is an instrumental that showcased his excellent guitar playing ability.

Magic Sam recorded a vocal rendition of "All Your Love" for the Cobra Label His piercing high voice was similar to that of Otis Rush. Magic Sam was a carbon copy of Jimi Hendrix. Unfortunately, Sam was stricken with a fatal heart attack in 1969. The younger generation of blues singers, those born in the 1930s and 1940s were deeply entrenched with soul music. Z.Z. Hill was born in 1941 copied the soul style of Bobby 'Blue' Bland and was accepted by the white audiences with his recording of "Down Home Blues" in 1981. Three years later, Z.Z. Hill was dead in 1984.

Jackie Wilson was born on June 9, 1934 in Detroit, Michigan. In his early teens he formed a quartet and called it the Ever Ready Gospel Singers. In 1951, Johnny Otis discovered that Jackie had talent while singing with a group called the Thrillers. They later changed their name to the Royals. In 1953, Jackie replaced Clyde McPhatter and sang the lead part in Billy Ward's Dominoes. Their big hit was "You Can't Keep a Good Man Down," and followed with another hit with "Rags to Riches."

In 1957, Wilson left the Dominoes to begin a solo career. His hits as a solo artist are, "To Be Loved," "That's Why," "I'll be Satisfied," and "(Your Love Keeps Lifting Me) Higher and Higher." On January 21, 1984 at the age of 49, Jackie Wilson died from a massive heart attack.

During the 1960s, James Copeland, born in 1937 was touring the circuit with Percy Mayfield and Freddie King singing his selections of soul, blues and rock music. The two decades of the 1960s and 1970s have produced many outstanding soul music performers. There were, James Brown, Ray Charles, Aretha Franklin, Stevie Wonder, the Supremes, Otis Redding, the Temptations, Wilson Pickett, Esther Phillips, Percy Sledge, Sam Cooke, Little Richard, Elmore James, Lowell Fulson, Ike and Tina Turner and countless others. Although they were categorized as soul performers, they also recorded other forms of music, such as, gospel, rhythm and blues, rock, jazz, popular music and blues. Soul music like the blues gave the artists the opportunity to express their innermost feelings in song.

12

WHITE BLUES (SKIFFLE) ZYDECO

When the field recording units were setting up their equipment, the engineers and talent scouts like Frank Walker representing Columbia Records, John and Alan Lomax, father and son for the Library of Congress and Polk Brockman for Okeh Records were getting ready for a full days work of recording for their companies. Sitting side by side waiting their turn to either sing or play their blues were both the blacks and the whites. This was about the closest relationship the two races would have in common. They all wanted to be heard on records.

On the particular day during the early 1920s in Atlanta, Georgia, two young white brothers from Tennessee, Austin and Lee Allen came up to the microphone with their guitar and banjo tuned to its accurate pitch, sang what became the biggest blues hits for Columbia Records, they were, "Chattanooga Blues," "Coal Mine Blues," and "Laughin' and Crying Blues."

When the day had ended, Frank Walker had waxed masters of ballads, ragtime songs, coon songs, novelty songs, dance music and the blues. But it was primarily the white country blues that they were focusing on for the white audiences out there. During the 1920s, there was an abundance of white blues available. Among them was Jimmie Rodgers, the White Country Blues Yodeler. The first country recorded instrumentalist was violinist Eck Robertson's version of "Arkansas Traveler" for Victor Records. Okeh Records had Frank Hutchinson's "Cannonball Blues."

Fiddlin' John Carson and his daughter Rosa Lee (Moonshine Kate) was the first country blues vocal of "Little Old Log Cabin in the Lane" for Okeh Records. Former Governor of Louisiana, Jimmie Davis, recorded a hokum version of "Down at the Country Church" for Victor Records in 1931. Another form of white blues was "Talking Blues," where the performer spoke the lyrics against a rhythmic background rather than singing them. There was Chris Bouchillon's "Talking Blues" for Columbia Records in 1926. Other artists to follow this pattern were, Lonnie Glossom's "Arkansas Hard Luck Blues" in 1936 for the Conqueror Label and "Talking Dust Bowl Blues" by Woody Guthrie for the Victor Label in 1940. During the 1940s, Woody worked with popular black artists like Leadbelly, Brownie McGhee, Sonny Terry and Big Bill Broonzy in New York. Broonzy's blues played a major part in Bob Dylan's career in the 1960s.

The duo team of Tom Darby and Jimmie Tarlton were kept busy in the recording studios of three major companies between 1927 to 1933. Darby and Tarlton recorded "Birmingham Jain" and "Columbus Stockade Blues" that became a two sided hit for Columbia Records. Although the record sold more than two hundred thousand copies, all they received was a flat sum of $75.00 each. This was because of the insistence of Darby's influence over Tarlton to take the $75.00 rather than accept the royalty rate that would have awarded them thousands of dollars each.

In 1928, Columbia called in the duo for a back-up session for their previous hits. They recorded another hit a sequel called "Birmingham Jail No.2," backed with "Lonesome Road." In 1930, they gave Columbia two more country blues hits with "Traveling Yodel Blues" and "Heavy Hearted Blues." "Columbus Stockade Blues" became a country standard and in 1940 Jimmie Davis made a cover record on it and so did Willie Nelson and Danny Davis in the 1960s.

Some white performers took no offense to be listed on the 'race' records along with the blacks. There was Salvatore Massaro also known as Eddie Lang, who played guitar duets with black Lonnie Johnson on "Have to Change Keys to Play These Blues," and a "Handful of Riffs" for the Okeh Label. Eddie also worked with blues singers, Texas Alexander, Bessie Smith, Coot Grant, Gladys Bently and Sox Wilson. Pianist Frank Melrose recorded "Whoopee Stomp" using the name 'Broadway Rastus for Paramount's 'race' label. Jazz guitarist George Barnes worked with Charlie McCoy, Blind John Davis, Jazz Gillum, Merline Johnson and Washboard Sam.

Emmett Miller is among the most influential white country singers in his day. Commonly known for his blackface vaudeville act, he recorded many hits for the Okeh Record Company. Among them were, "The Licker Taster," "Lovesick Blues" and "Anytime" in the 1920s. He also recorded "St. Louis Blues" and "I Ain't Got Nobody" with jazz musicians, Tommy Dorsey, Gene Krupa and Edie Lang. in 1928. Many white blues singers looked to Blind Lemon Jefferson to emulate. Most noticeable was Larry Hensley's "Match Box Blues" recorded in 1934 on the Vocalion Label.

When Jimmie Rodger's "Blue Yodel" for Victor and Darby and Tarlton's "Columbus Stockade Blues" for Columbia became financial successes, the other major labels went on a campaign to recruit white blues artists available. Gennett Records found Gene

Autry, Howard Keesee, Bill Bruner and Jerry Behrens went with Okeh Records while Bluebird got Daddy John Love and Jesse Rodgers

During the 1930s, the fiddle was the main instrument of the white country blues. One prominent fiddler was Willie T. Narmour from Mississippi who recorded two big hits for Okeh Records with his guitarist Shellie Smith, the songs were, "Carroll Country Blues" and "Charleston No. 1." Then there was G.B. Grayson, a fiddler from Tennessee who preferred to write his songs about trains. For Victor Records he recorded "Train 45" and "Going down the Lee Highway." Tommy Magness, a Georgia fiddler often played with Bill Monroe, Roy Acuff, Arthur Smith and Roy Hall and his Blue Ridge Entertainers. Kirk McGhee an outstanding blues fiddler was very popular in the late 1920s with his Vocalion hits of; "Salt Lake City Blues,"" Salty Dog Blues" and "Milkcow Blues."

In the 1950s white country musicians were more active playing the blues than any other form of music. Monroe 'Moe' Jackson recorded "Go 'Way from My Door" for the Mercury Label in 1951. 'Harmonica Frank' Floyd from Tucapola, Mississippi who was inspired by the music of Blind Boy Fuller, recorded "Step It Up and Go" and "Howlin' Tom Cat" for Chess Records in 1951. Then in 1954 he did "Rockin' Chair Daddy" for Sun Records. The most prominent white country singer to come from Tupelo, Mississippi was Elvis Presley. In his early recording years for Sun Records, Elvis made cover records of the blues artists in the past. His "That's All Right" was Arthur 'Big Boy' Crudup's blues. "Good Rockin' Tonight" was previously recorded by Roy Brown and Wynonie Harris and the "Milkcow Blues Boogie" was from Kokomo Arnold. Following Presley's footsteps were Jerry Lee Lewis, Eddie Cochran, Gene Vincent, Carl Perkins and the Everly Brothers who included the blues in their repertoire.

During the 1950s and 1960s, 'Skiffle' bands became very popular in England. An example of a skiffle band was that of Lonnie Donigan's Rock Island Line" for Decca Records in 1955.

A skiffle band consisted of a washboard, kazoo, jug, washtub bass, drums, acoustic guitar and harmonica. Skiffle bands made their appearance in the United States in New York's Greenwich Village and in coffee houses, blues clubs and at rent parties. Eventually, bands of this type did not last very long; they soon gave way for the incoming 'beat' generation and rock and roll.

In the 1960s more white groups became involved with the blues. There were the Grateful Dead, the Jefferson Airplanes, Canned Heat, Janis Joplin, Captain Beefhart and Big Brother and the Holding Company. The appeal of the blues was evident by the interest of these white performers. Unfortunately, when the white blues became popular, it put the black blues artists on the back burner temporarily, at least until the blues revival, when they would be re-discovered again.

Zydeco music is probably the only form of black blues that has been influenced by white music. Zydeco or Zodico as it is sometimes called is a dance type music established by the British in the 18th century. Originating in Nova Scotia by the Arcadians who left their homeland and traveled south to settle in Louisiana. After centuries of intermarriages between French Arcadians, the Indians and the blacks, their off springs became known as "Cajuns." Cajun or Zydeco music is usually played with guitar, fiddle, button accordion and a washboard. Its earliest recordings date back to 1934 when John Lomax recorded Ellis Evans playing harmonica and Jimmie Lewis on washboard with Austin Coleman or Washington Brown doing the vocals.

During the 1940s, Alton 'Rockin' Dopsie' Rubin, an outstanding zydeco musician formed a group called Zydeco Twisters featuring talented musicians as Saxophonist John Hart, Guitar Slim, Jimmy Rogers and Little Richard toured the south to acquaint the public of the 'new' style of dancing music. Leadbelly, an accomplished button accordionist recorded "Corn Bread Rough," an up-tempo dance theme in 1942 for the Asch Label. During the decades of the 1940s and 1950s, blues began to intermingle with the popular black Cajun music. It was however,

Clifford Chenier, born in Louisiana in 1925 who was the first to develop the style of Zydeco in its Blues-Cajun form. Chenier, regarded as the undisputed "King of Zydeco Music" recorded 'Cliston Blue" on the Elko Label in 1954 with his cousin Morris 'Big' Chenier on guitar and Clifton playing button accordion. Then in 1955, Chenier recorded several hits that gained him national distribution for his record sales.

Clifton along with his brother Cleveland playing the metal chest washboard recorded a rocking instrumental called, "Hot Rod" on the Arhoolie Label followed with his biggest hit "Louisiana Blues" and Blake Snake Blues," and "I'm A Hog For You" on the same session. In 1975, Chenier put together one of the finest zydeco bands that included his brother Cleveland on washboard and John Hart on saxophone. The band not only recorded smash hits including, "Rockin' Accordion," "Black Gal," "Tu Le Ton Son Ton," "Monifique" and "Jambalaya" but was also the featured band at the 1975 Montreux Jazz Festival in Switzerland. In 1957, his son C. J. Chenier was born on September 28, in Port Arthur, Texas. At a very early age, he took to playing the trumpet and accordion. After several years of constant practicing and playing with local bands, C.J. joined the Red Hot Louisiana Band.

Taking advantage of his father's popularity, C.J. took leadership of the group and re-named it the New Red Hot Louisiana Band. After an extensive tour throughout the south to build up a following for their music, Arhoolie Records called them in to record their first album, "Let Me in Your Heart," which featured a song that he wrote as a tribute to his father called "Check out the Zydeco."

During the 1940s and the mid-1950s, blues gradually began to mingle with the black Cajun music and the combination led to a blend of Zydeco. Clarence Garlow's "Let the Good Times Roll" and "Paper in My Shoe" by Wilson 'Boozoo' Chavis are good examples of this marriage between the blues and Cajun music. Other zydeco performers deserving mention are; Stanley

'Buckwheat' Doral, Conray Fontenot, Sidney Babineaux Albert Chevalier, Marcel Dugas, Wild Bill Pitre, Lawrence 'Black' Ardoin and Bois-Sec Ardoin.

13

BLUES PROGRESSIONS & BLUES SCALE

After the Emancipation, musical instruments were used to accompany the blues. The more commonly used instruments were the harmonica, banjo and guitar. It was however, the guitar that the blues singers preferred for accompaniment because it provided a greater effect and background in their singing. Gradually, the blues became an instrumental form of music. No longer limited to vocal music. Musicians could play the blues on their instruments.

With the passing of time, Negroes were slowly being introduced to brass and reed musical instruments. They taught themselves to play blues and jazz on these new European imports.

Many blacks learned to master these instruments, yet they still had the urge to sing a line in their musical breaks. But when more and more musicians mastered their instruments, the blues began to change. Trumpeter Louis Armstrong and pianist Jelly Roll Morton were great blues singers as well as master of their instruments. The creation and development of the blues was mainly accomplished by illiterate musicians and singers who by the majority could not read music. Therefore, they had to improvise around a preset musical pattern. The most familiar pattern at the time was the twelve bar blues with a precise designated harmonic progression that was easily committed to the musicians memory. The early blues form was very simply written requiring the three basic chord changes. They are the I-IV-V chords. The structure of the blues is simple and is mostly used in a twelve bar pattern with the I-IV-V chord progressions played at predetermined measures. They are, four bars of the I chord, two bars of the IV chord, two bars of the I chord, two bars of the V7 chord and two bars of the I chord. This is the exact original basic blues progression. (See example 1).

Example 1

Originally, the blues was a personal and individual expression of feelings. It could be about a certain event, or an experience they had, or perhaps some form of hardship they had to endure or about every day life in general. Slavery, for example, provided lyrics for many blues people. The men sang about the inhumane treatment they received under the master's whip. The women sang about the many rapes and sexual acts they had to perform to both the slave master and sometimes to his wife or mistress. These were the lyrics associated with the early or primitive blues.

However, W. C. Handy, around the early 1900s saw the commercial value of the blues and began to update and modify the blues progressions. Gradually, the placement of the I-IV-V chords began to change in their location within the twelve bar blues pattern. Today we find a complete change of the harmonic structure of the blues as we can see in examples 2 through 19. Example 20 is an eight bar blues progression.

Basically, there are only six notes to a blues scale. They are arranged in the order of a minor third, a major second, a minor second, a minor second, a minor third and a major second. The following illustration shows the construction on the blues scale in all twelve keys.

Example 21

From the beginning of the twentieth century, African-Americans have used the blues to express their feelings in song that had played a major influence in their culture.

The country blues was the first type of blues to be identified. Its lyrics were primarily focused on sexual relationships. Women selling sex.

Buddy Bolden, king of the trumpet players, was known to play "low-down" blues' Jelly Roll Morton although known to be ragtime and jazz pianist was very much at home playing the blues. Lil Hardin, the noted jazz pianist with King Oliver's band and later to become Mrs. Louis Armstrong was also recognized as a great blues player. Lucille Hegamin whom Mamie Smith referred to as a singer of the blues recorded her biggest blues hit "Arkansas Blues" with the accompaniment of the Blue Flame Syncopaters which was released on eleven different record labels

14

RHYTHM AND BLUES

Rhythm and blues was the phrase that came into use in 1949 as a replacement for the earlier term 'race records.' Race records was the accepted expression for all recordings by black artists that began in 1920 with Mamie Smith's hit "Crazy Blues". In its June 25, 1949 issue, Billboard's music trade magazine announced that the term 'race' would be terminated and replaced with rhythm and blues. This new expression was the accepted term for the American blacks during the 1950s and 1960s. Rhythm and blues was primarily ensemble music, a notable contrast to that of the blues. Usually a solo vocalist, a vocal group or an instrumentalist would provide the melody with a rhythm section of piano, bass, guitar and drums supplying the rhythmic background.

During the era of the classic blues songsters, it was the major record companies like Columbia, Victor, Bluebird, Okeh and Decca that monopolized the recording industry. But from the late 1940s onward the smaller black owned record companies that started in the southern cities of Memphis, Nashville and Houston took over control of rhythm and blues recordings. Eventually, small companies were springing up on the West Coast and into northern citied like Chicago, Detroit, Newark, Philadelphia and New York.

Big Joe Turner was among the first of the blues singers to get on the band-wagon of rhythm and blues when he recorded "Shake, Rattle and Roll" in April 1954 for Atlantic Records. A hit that remained on the R&B charts for over six months. But in June of that year, a young ambitious white musician named Bill Haley recorded it and took the limelight away from Big Joe Turner's version. In 1955, Turner was again up-staged by white performers who preferred to do a cover record on his tunes. Pat Boone recorded Turner's first hit for Atlantic Records, "Chains of Love" and following Big Joe's "Shake, Rattle and Roll" was "Flip, Flop and Fly" recorded by Johnny Ray.

Blues singer Lonnie Johnson recorded "Careless Love" in 1928, and 40 years later he re-recorded it for the R&B charts which Elvis Presley did a cover on the tune as a tribute to Lonnie. Muddy Waters in the early 1950s had several hits that were listed in the R&B charts. Among them were; "Long Distance Call" and "Honey Bee." Lowell Fulson's 1949 hit of "Three O'clock Blues" was later recorded by B.B. King in 1951 and took full credit for the success of that tune. T-Bone Walker, Pee Wee Crayton, Pete Lewis, Willie Dixon's trio with Ollie Crawford on guitar and pianist Leonard 'Baby Doo' Caston joined the ranks to rhythm and blues.

Rhythm and blues embraced various types of the blues and blues related music. Fats Domino, Chuck Berry, Little Richard, Bo Diddley and Louis Jordan with his first number one R&B hit of "Blue Light Boogie" were among the first to expose R&B to the public. Unlike the blues that often described troubled times and hardships, rhythm and blues was happy dancing music. It was heard in black American churches. Black bands during the 'swing era' were playing rhythm and blues, bands like Johnny Otis, Count Basie and Lionel Hampton

During the early 1950s, B.B. King, Bobby 'Blue' Bland, Roscoe Gordon and Jackie Brenston were recording R&B tunes. Johnnie Ray's "Cry" and Eddie Boyd's "Five Long Years" hit the top of the R&B chart. Vocal groups were heavy into R&B. There were the "Crew Cuts," Billy Ward and the Dominoes, the Orioles, the Drifters. The Moon glows and the Crows. A good deal of R&B came from gospel music. The hymn "Stand by Me" by Ben E. King was an R&B classic.

In 1956, Big Maybelle who grew up as a singer in the Jackson Sanctified Church choir in Mississippi joined the staff of black artists on the Savoy Records in Newark, New Jersey. She recorded one hit after another on the R&B chart, there were, "Grabbin' Blues," "My Country Man," "Way Back Home" and her biggest hit "Candy." With the wide spread interest in black music, the white entertainers decided to capitalize on its popularity. During the 1950s and into the 1960s, white performers made cover records previously recorded by blacks. For instance, it was Willie Mae Thornton who first recorded "Hound Dog" that was later recorded by Elvis Presley. The Crew Cuts made a cover record on the Chords R&B hit "Sh-Boom," The Chords also recorded the "Wheel of Fortune" that was followed by Kay Starr's version. Peggy Lee with the Benny Goodman orchestra did a successful cover record on Lil Green's hit "Fever." And the list could go on and on. Rhythm and blues played a major role in the continuation of the blues. It was also the stepping stone for the next development of the blues, that of Rock and Roll. The 1950s saw the emergence of another trend of the blues. In 1969, rhythm and blues was replaced by soul music.

15

ROCK 'N' ROLL

When Jackie Brenston recorded "Rocket 88" on the Chess Label, it became a number one hit on the R&B chart in 1951. This version was an indication of what the sound of rock 'n' roll would be. Some music theorist referred to it as being the first rock 'n' roll record. Alan Freed, a white disc jockey from Cleveland, Ohio who later moved his operations to New York, was credited for coining the phrase Rock 'N' Roll. Rhythm and blues and country-western styles became the main ingredients for rock music.

The official date of rock 'n' roll's beginning was in 1955, when "Rock Around the Clock" was recorded by Bill Haley and the Comets. The song was introduced as the principle theme music in the picture "Blackboard Jungle." The record became an instrumental success with its popularity in the United States and Europe. There were however, similar types of 'rock' music that were recorded by Bill Haley and the Comets, such as, "Crazy, Man, Crazy" in 1953 and "Dim Dim the Lights," in 1954. Joe Turner's "Shake, Rattle, and Roll," "Gee" by the Crows, "Sh-Boom" by the Chords, and the Midnighter's "Work With Me Annie." But what made "Rock Around The Clock" the turning point for rock 'n' roll was the major record company's involvement in the 'new' music craze and began to inundate the white record buying public in America and Europe.

The format for 'rock' music was the typical twelve bar blues pattern with several improvised chorus' of the theme by an instrumentalist, usually a saxophone or a trumpet, in addition to the solo singer or a vocal group. The rock 'n' roll era gave the black artists the opportunity to get exposure in the white market. There were, Chuck Berry's "Maybelline," Tutti Frutti," by Little Richard, Bo Diddley's version of "Bo Diddley," Earth Angel," by the Penguins and the "Great Pretender" by the Platters. Then in 1956, Elvis Presley stole the spot light away from all other artists with successful recordings of, "Heartbreak Hotel," "Hound Dog," "Love Me Tender," and "Blue Suede Shoes." In 1957, it was "Jailhouse Rock," "All shook Up," and "Let Me Be Your Teddy Bear."

The rock 'n' roll period divided the performers into various groups. The black artists, like Fats Domino, Chuck Berry, Bo Diddley, and Little Richard were singing in the black style of rhythm and blues. Elvis Presley, Jerry Lee Lewis, Buddy Holly and Bill Haley would combine the rhythm and blues with their southern white country music in their performances. While most of the music performed by these artists was up-tempo, there were other solo artists and vocal groups that preferred the slower less rhythmic sound, such as, Bobby Darin, Pat Boone, Paul Anka and Ricky Nelson. The vocal groups were the Drifters, the Penguins, the Coasters, and the Clovers. These performers preferred to use the standard 32 bar form of music (AABA) rather than the 12 bar blues pattern.

As rock continued to develop into the 1960s, other forms of music were taking shape. There was the "Twist," made popular by Chubby Checker. Around the mid- 1960s, the European groups of the Beatles and the Rolling Stones came to America causing what some music writers called the England invasion. The "Motown Sound," was created by such artists as, the Supremes, Marvin Gaye, Martha and the Vandellas, the Spinners, Gladys Knight and the Pips and many more.

The Mamas and the Papas, the Byrds and Bob Dylan introduced "Folk Rock" in 1965. The following year in 1966, the Jefferson Airplanes gave us "Acid" or "Psychedelic Rock." The 1970s revealed many types of rock music. There were the combinations of gospels, blues and jazz with rock music. The 1980s gave us the outstanding instrumental groups as, Chicago, Blood, Sweat and Tears, and Weather Report, whose music was a blend of jazz-rock and a touch of the blues. Also in this decade were "Reggae" and "Rap." Reggae, the African-Caribbean music combined with American rhythm and blues came from the ghettos of the black sections of major cities. It is still going strong in the mid-1990s.

16

1960s REVIVAL OF THE BLUES

Europe in the 1960s saw a massive invasion of blues artists from the past. The purpose of the trip abroad was to rekindle the flame and re-activate the spirit of the Europeans view of the blues and the Americans. Among the first to leave the United States were Willie Dixon and Memphis Slim who were embarking for their tour throughout Europe and the Middle East. Brownie McGhee and Sonny Terry along with Eddie Boyd, Curtis Jones and the Champion Jack Dupree were there to give the blues a revival or as the media called it a rebirth.

Slowly, the blues was catching on again, but the new young enthusiast wanted to hear and see in person the older blues performers. So there became a re-discovery of 'Son' House, John

Hurt, Mance Lipscomb, Fred McDowell, Robert Pete Williams, Robert Shaw, Bukka White, Sleepy John Estes and others. When they were on tour in Europe, it was always a sold out audience. The bluesmen captured the hearts of the Europeans and managed to keep that momentum going for future blues artists ready to appear on the scene. By the mid-1960s, the Folk Blues Festival brought Howlin' Wolf, John Lee Hooker and 'Sonny Boy' Williamson to Europe where British groups like the Rolling Stones, Alexis Korner and Cyril Davies who fashioned their music after the bluesmen of America.

Another important reason why the blacks invaded Europe in the 1960s was because there was work for them in the nightclubs and concert tours. Willie Dixon summed it all up when he told a reporter, "I wouldn't have gone over there in the first place had I been doing all right here, you know." During the American Folk-Blues Festival on tour in Europe, many of the English pop artists took note of the popularity of the blues that was spreading throughout their homeland. It wasn't long before they were recording songs of the black bluesmen. The Rolling Stones, the Yardbirds and other groups were doing Willie Dixon's songs.

England was the center of attraction for blues-rock. Records of B.B. King or Bobby 'Blue' Bland could be heard on the local radio stations and on the juke boxes in taverns, juke joints and on records. Many white youngsters got acquainted with the blues by listening to Jimi Hendrix, Paul Butterfield and John Mayall's Blues breakers or by listening to soul artists like, Aretha Franklin, Jackie Wilson and Jimmy Hughes. Likewise, rock 'n' roll fans got a taste of the blues through Chuck Berry, Bo Diddley, Jerry Lee Lewis and Fats Domino. Much of the blues records were played on the pop radio stations that had a listening audience of young black and white kids as well as their parents.

Influential in the 1960s revival of the blues was Jimmy Reed. Calvin Carter, a representative of the Vee-Jay Record Company heard Jimmy play harmonica and guitar in Chicago and invited him to a record session. "High and Lonesome," and "Roll and Rhumba" were Reed's first record that made a local hit because Vee-Jay was not fully equipped for national distribution. Jimmy's blues were of the happy lyrical type and also with a rhythm that kids could dance to. Although Jimmy was primarily a bluesman, much of his music was categorized as rock 'n' roll along with Fats Domino and Chuck Berry. Reed was well liked and respected by the other artists. His health took a turn for the worst with his problems with alcohol and Epilepsy. Jimmy died in 1976 at the age of 51.

Muddy Waters, Howlin' Wolf, Memphis Slim, 'Sonny Boy' Williamson and John Lee Hooker were among the rediscovered of the 1960s revival. In 1964, Chess Records released Muddy's folk-blues albums, "Folk Singer," "The Real Folk-Blues" and "More Real Folk-Blues." Many of Howlin' Wolf, Memphis Slim and 'Sonny Boy's' singles were reissued to a financial success. In addition to the re-birth of the prominent blues artists of the past, the revival was also a period for the sidemen in the band to be discovered. From the Muddy Waters band came, Otis Spann, James Cotton, and Walter (Shakey) Horton became solo artists and was called into the recording studios to produce several outstanding albums.

In 1960, Willie Dixon took guitarist George 'Buddy' Guy into Chess Records where 'Buddy' remained until 1967 recording session after session as a solo artist and also as a supporting guitarist for other Chess artists like, Little Walter, 'Sonny Boy' Williamson, Koko Taylor, Howlin' Wolf, Muddy Waters and others. Buddy has been an inspiration to other guitarist as Eddie Van Halen, Stevie Ray Vaughn, Jeff Beck and Carlos Santana. In the 1970s and 1980s he toured with harpist Junior Wells and also made an indelible mark with Jimi Hendrix and Eric Clapton who remarked that Buddy was ,"The best guitar player alive." In 1990, Buddy received a Grammy award for his album of "Damn Right, I've Got the Blues," and "Feels like Rain." Today, Guy is more popular than he ever was and is constantly traveling abroad to perform with Eric Clapton, Jeff Beck and Junior Wells.

Blues guitarist Earl Hooker, cousin to John Lee Hooker was discovered by Willie Dixon in the late 1960s and recorded several albums before his demise in 1970. Jimmy Dawkins, Luther Allison and Johnny Little John were among the new talents of the blues revival in the 1960s. The rebirth of former blues artists were Robert Nighthawk, Sunnyland Slim, Eddie Taylor, Billy Boy Arnold and Johnny Shines. But it was Otis Rush, Freddy King, Magic Sam and Buddy Guy who were the most prominent.

Chicago already acclaimed as the blues capital was now beginning to lose its musicians for others parts of the country. During the 1960s, the blues became active in St. Louis, Houston, Oakland, Detroit and Los Angeles. Relocating on the west coast were white musicians Paul Butterfield, Charlie Musselwhite, Elvin Bishop and Mike Bloomfield. The black musicians to depart from Chicago were Freddie Roulette, Luther Ticker and Shakey Jake. The American Folk-Blues Festival in the 1960s did much to expose blues artists as Big Joe Turner, T-Bone Walker and Lonnie Johnson. As the revival movement spilled over into the 1970s, it was the women who were re-discovered, they include, Victoria Spivey, Elizabeth Cotton, Etta James, Alberta Hunter, 'Sippie' Wallace, Viola Wells, Koko Taylor, Edith Wilson and Helen Humes.

Victoria Spivey was recording her new songs on her own Spivey Label along with Lucille Hegamin and Hannah Sylvester. Edith Wilson was doing the Quaker Oaks commercial and was performing in the blues clubs and the festival circuits until she passed away in 1981. 'Sippie' Wallace made her 1980s hit with "Women, Be Wise." During the 1960s attention was focused on a handful of outstanding guitarist, they were, Otis Rush, Buddy Guy, Freddie King, Albert King and B.B. King (no relations between the three of them).

Otis Rush enjoyed a revival success with Chess Records with his classic "So Many Roads." Freddie King had two successful instrumentals on the King/Federal Label with "High Away" and "San-ho-zay" followed with "Surf Monkey," "The

Stumble and Bossa Nova Watusii Twist." Albert King who idolized B.B. King did his best to emulate his style of playing and singing. His "Blues at Sunrise" on Stax Records was rated among the best seller in 1969.

Percy Mayfield, born on August 12, 1920 in Minden, Louisiana began his music career at a very early age. During his high school years, he participated in all the school's musicals, writing poetry and songs for the plays. In his early twenties, his professional career began when he presented "Two Years of Torture" a song he had composed for Jimmy Witherspoon who was recording for Supreme Records. But when the executives of Supreme heard Percy's demonstration of the song, they suggested that he record it instead of Witherspoon. With the musical backing of outstanding studio musicians such as saxophonist Maxwell Davis and guitarist Chuck Norris, the record became a big hit on the west coast.

In 1950, Specialty Records recorded Percy's biggest number one hit, "Please, Send Me Someone to Love." Percy's songwriting career was skyrocketing. Everything he did was a success. Record companies were vying for his talent. He recorded for Brunswick, Supreme, Specialty, R.C.A., Atlantic, Cash and 7Arts records. All of Percy's songs were recorded by the top recording artists like Robert Nighthawk, Little Junior Parker, Lovie Lee, Shirley Scott, B.B. King, Lou Rawls, Dinah Washington and Ray Charles. Out of his pen came songs like, "River Invitation," "The Bottle Is My Companion," "Hit The Road Jack, " "Two Years of Torture," "Please, Send Me Someone To Love," "My Jug and I," and many more.

Ray Charles was so impressed with Percy Mayfield's songwriting talents that he signed him to a five year contract to write at least twelve songs a year for Ray to record. "Hit the Road Jack" was a successful hit for Ray Charles. Then In August, 1952 Percy was involved in a serious car accident when he was returning back to Los Angeles after doing several shows in Las Vegas. His driver smashed into the rear of a slow moving vehicle that nearly took Percy's life. Badly disfigured, Percy refrained from making any public appearances.

During this depressive period in his life, Percy took to heavy drinking, which brought on his first heart attack in 1972. His devoted wife Tina was his main support to slow him down on his drinking and get him back to his true love-music. Gradually, Percy began performing in public and did several record sessions. Then on August 11, 1984, Percy had another heart attack and died in his wife's arms. A great talent lost to the world. Percy was labeled, "The Poet Laureate of the Blues."

Lowell Fulson was born in Tulsa, Oklahoma in 1921 and started playing the guitar at an early age; Lowell developed into a skillful guitarist and was constantly called upon to back up other artists on their records. Having an excellent singing voice he recorded his first record for the Big Town Label, "Crying Blues" in 1946. In 1950, Lowell experienced his first big hit with "Blue Shadows" that landed number one on the R&B chart. This was followed with another big seller on "Everyday I Have the Blues" in 1950. Two years later with the Count Basie Band Joe Williams did a cover record on the tune. Lowell's popularity grew with the public. Big Town Records recorded his "Come Back Baby" and "Three O'clock Blues" was recorded on the Trilon Label. Lowell traveled the European circuit with his band promoting his music. After taking a hiatus from the music business for several years, he was re-discovered during the 1960s revival period. Lowell Fulson is listed among the greatest of all bluesmen. He died in 1999 at the age of 78.

B.B. King from Mississippi was a born bluesman from the start. In his early years, he would stand on street corners in his town of Itta Bena, playing and singing for whatever change people passing by would give him. By the time he was twenty-two years old in 1947; he left his hometown and traveled north along Highway 55 to Memphis. B.B. stayed with his cousin Bukka White who introduced him to 'Sonny Boy' Williamson. In 1948, King was given a chance to perform on Williamson's radio show on

Station KWEM which brought on more offers to participate on the radio. It wasn't long after that when the club owners were offering King a spot in their clubs.

In 1949, King got a contract to record for a small local record company called Bullet and recorded his first release of "Miss Martha King," dedicated to his first wife. After Bullet Records, King moved on to a larger company called Modern Records where he recorded "She's Dynamite" in 1950. Then in 1951 on the RPM Label, B.B. recorded "Three O'clock Blues," it was with the success of this record where it hit number one on the R&B charts in February, 1952, that B.B. King got his well deserved recognition. In 1955, King put together a full time band and went on the road as he is still doing today. In 1961, King signed with ABC-Paramount Records to get better distribution on his records and more money on royalties. B.B. was moving right along with the wave of his popularity. He appeared on stage as the opening act for the Rolling Stones. He made appearances on the Tonight Show, the Ed Sullivan Show, and worked in the lounge at Caesars Palace in Las Vegas. There was no stopping B.B. King, he was on a roll. In the 1990s, he was inducted into the Blues Foundation Hall of Fame and the Rock 'n' Roll Hall of Fame.

The years from 1960 to 1970 saw the passing away of some notable blues greats. They were, Elmore James (1963), Armenter Chatman (Bo Carter-1964), 'Sonny Boy' Williamson (1965), Joshua Barnes 'Peg Leg' Howell (1966), Ida Cox and Robert Nighthawk (1967), 'Little Walter' Jacobs and James Kokomo Arnold (1968), Samuel Machett (Magic Sam) and Joshua Daniel 'Josh' White (1969), Otis Spann and Lonnie Johnson (1970).

Since the 1960s revival of the blues and a re-birth and the revival in the 1980s, it is evident that the blues have a prominent position in the music entertainment. The blues has made its recovery against all the opposition from the Rhythm and Blues and Rock 'n' Roll people. The blues people are saying "We are here to stay, and as long as we have singers to sing the blues, we will be like the flame that will never blow out.

17

BLUES IN EUROPE

Europe was introduced to the blues by their white performers such as the skiffle bands that originated out of England and the young groups of the Rolling Stones, the Who, the Yardbirds, the Animals, the Beatles, Fleetwood Mac, Eric Clapton and others. During the blues revival of the 1960s, it was however, the black blues people from the United States who went to Europe to re-activate the spirit and interest of the blues to the Europeans. Among them were, Willie Dixon, Memphis Slim, T-Bone Walker, John Lee Hooker, Sonny Terrell, Big Joe Williamson, Buddy Guy and a host of others.

Alex 'Rice' Miller (Sonny Boy) Williamson was a local favorite in Memphis, Tennessee, but did not reach his true recognition until he traveled to Europe. In 1961, he recorded "Nine below Zero" with his guitarist Robert Lockwood, Jr. for the Checker Label. And in 1963, he went on tour in Europe with his release of "On My Way Back Home," and was immediately accepted by the European public.

In the 1920s, professional women blues singers, Alberta Hunter, Ethel Waters, Gertrude Saunders, Beulah 'Sippie' Wallace and others made an impact with the blues while on tour and in concerts in Europe where the all black shows were warmly accepted. When John Hammond contracted Bessie Smith to do what became her last recording session in 1933, it was for the Parlophone Label in England. The main song that came out of that session was "Nobody Knows You When You're Down And Out."

In 1949, Leadbelly took his show to France. It was such a financial success that other European countries wanted the blues artists to perform for their people. In 1951, Big Bill Broonzy traveled throughout Europe featuring his popular hits of, "John Henry" and "Black, Brown and White." There was no end of the influx of black blues performers for Europe. England was blessed with the talents of Muddy Waters, Otis Spann, Sonny Terry and Brownie McGhee in 1958. It took a little while for the Europeans to get acquainted with Muddy Waters' electric guitar, since they were accustomed to the acoustic guitar sound. But, after hearing Muddy's masterful performance on his guitar it was widely accepted.

The re-birth of the blues in Europe was obvious that music magazine were paying more attention to it and giving full coverage in their articles about the blues people and their music. Music critics, Yannick Bruynoghe and George Adins of Belgium and French writers Marcel Chauvard and Jacques Demetre came to the United States to do more research of the blues and its people. They settled in Chicago and Detroit for numerous interviews for information about the blues music, the clubs where blues were performed and the lifestyle of the blues people themselves.

With the growth and expansion of the blues in Europe, many publishers were printing blues magazines for their growing market, there were, "Blue Unlimited," "Blues World," and

"Rhythm and Blues Monthly" from England. Belgium had, "R&B Panorama" and Sweden published the "Jefferson" magazine. Germany, France, Japan, Italy and Finland had their editions of blues magazines. There was a hunger for more information about the blues and its people. Sweden sent Bengt Olsson to research the medicine shows and the fife and drum bands. Researchers came to the Carolinas, Louisiana, Mississippi, Chicago, Detroit and Alabama to learn more about their musical traditions.

While on a European tour, Sleepy John Estes, Yank Rachel and Hammie Nixon recorded "Rats in My Kitchen" and "Easin' Back to Tennessee" in 1962. Son House performed for the European public from 1964 to 1970. In 1965, Son House recorded "Empire State Express" for Columbia Records, but his failing health took its toll and he was forced to retire by the mid-1970s.

The Rolling Stones patterned their style of music with that of the Louisiana Blues. Several British musicians like Alexis Korner and Cyril Davies copied the style of guitarist Snapper Blackwell, Leroy Carr's duo partner. The results were their experimental version of "Down Home" rural blues as could be heard in their recording of "Blue Mink" on the Ace of Hearts Label in 1963. The Rolling Stones further developed their style into the form of rock-blues with an excellent rendition of "Little Red Rooster" recorded in 1964 for Decca Records. The outstanding guitarist Eric Clapton demonstrated his mastery of the instrument on the 1966 Decca release of "All Your Love" with John Mayall's Blues Breakers. In 1960, Memphis Slim left the United States to take up residence in Europe. He recorded in Paris and was treated royally. He was well received in all the clubs and concerts while on tour and had no intentions of ever coming back to the United States. He did not take kindly to how the black bluesmen were treated in America.

In 1949, Leadbelly was one of the first bluesmen to tour France and other countries in Europe. It was during this tour that the groundwork was laid for the blues revival in the 1960s. The Europeans heard for the first time country blues, rural blues, urban blues and folk music as played and sung by Leadbelly. Big Bill Broonzy was England's favorite American artist. He was looked upon and idolized by British guitarist Keith Richards of the Rolling Stones and Martin Carthy. While on tour in Europe, Broonzy was a financial success and was greeted by an enthusiastic audience. He told Europeans that he was the last of the bluesmen in America.

In 1963, 'Rice' Miller 'Sonny Boy' Williamson was a tremendous hit in England. Young British groups like the Animals, and the Yardbirds looked up to 'Rice' Miller as their inspiration and 'Rice' even had them come in and record with him on his sessions while there. His last record date was in Copenhagen, Denmark for the Storyville Label in 1965. The session produced "Keep it to Ourselves" and "When the Lights Went Out." Shortly after the records were released, 'Sonny Boy' came back to America, as he told his friends, "I just came home to die." It happened in 1965.

During the 1960s revival, Europe got so involved with the blues and the blues people that they didn't want to wait for all the America blues artists to arrive there. So, England dispatched their music researcher Paul Oliver and his wife Valerie to the United States to get as much information and musical presentations as they could on tape to bring back home. While in Detroit, Oliver's first objective was the piano blues where he recorded Boogie-Woogie Red. Shortly afterwards, he traveled to Chicago and hooked up with pianist Eurreal 'Little Brother' Montgomery and Roosevelt Sykes for a one-on-one interview and a demonstration of their performance Sunnyland Slim and Otis Spann were also called upon for their input and demonstration on barrelhouse music and the blues.

Paul Oliver came in contact with blind guitarist James Brewer and Arvella Gray as they were playing on Chicago's Maxwell Street corners. Oliver recorded Gray's "Corinne Corinna" a barrelhouse composition and "Have Mercy Mr. Percy" a popular blues tune. Oliver's trip to the United States was successful. He got what he came for. He recorded Robert 'Junior' Lockwood, J.B.

Lenoir, Will Shade, Jasper Love, Robert Curtis Smith, Wade Walton and others. Loaded with tapes and documents, Oliver and his wife returned to England.

The American Folk Blues Festival and the Newport Folk Festival were other vehicles that brought the blues to Europe. Traveling with the folk festivals were, Brownie McGhee, Reverend Gary Davis, Sonny Terry, John Lee Hooker, John Hurt, Jesse Fuller and others. When word got back to America that Europe provided more opportunities for employment for the blues artists, there was a massive departure for Europe. Blacks were enjoying the enthusiastic welcome by the Europeans that many have stayed on after their concert tours were completed. They included, Memphis Slim, Eddie Boyd, Jack Dupree and Curtis Jones.

Europe however, was anxious to hear Sam 'Lightnin' Hopkins in concert and had offered him two thousand dollars a week for a tour to last as long as he wanted. But Sam had so much fear in flying that he refused the offer and remained in the United States to work in pool halls, juke joints and saloons for $17.00 a night. For the blues people who traveled to Europe, their rewards included prestige, popularity and the opportunity to work in more and in better clubs in the United States. The blues continues to prosper throughout Europe.

18

BLUES TODAY

Now, in the decade of the 2000s, the record companies now release CDs that are produced in advanced studios with its multi-tracking consoles that have as many as forty-eight individual tracks with built in echo chambers for the highest level of recording technology. Today's blues artists are quite familiar with the new recording studios. They can come in for a session and adjust themselves to the use of the sensitized microphones and the liquefied headphones. They can be completely enclosed in a glass chamber or a square cubicle and feel comfortable in these surroundings. Inside the booth or the control room sits the sound engineer, a technician and sometime the record producer to operate the sophisticated recording equipment.

This scenario however, came a long way from the earlier recording days. It was quickly noticed that when the talent scouts brought the itinerant blues artists into a big city recording studio that was unfamiliar to them, they found it difficult to adjust to the strange environment that they were tensed and uncomfortable; therefore they were not able to produce an acceptable session. So it was the task of the talent scouts to load the back of their cars with a complete set of recording equipment and bring the "studio" so to speak to the surroundings that the artists could relate to and feel comfortable with. This allowed them to sing and play their blues in a relaxed atmosphere, which was the beginning of the field recordings.

When the results of the field recordings were sent back to the major studios the record companies discovered that they have a product that they could produce for a special group of people. Since the artists were all black, the sales market would be targeted to the black community which gave birth to the term 'race' records. Blues was basically black people's music. It was composed, sung, played and recorded by blacks for their black audiences, but as the blues was gaining in popularity, the audiences began to expand and many white people came to hear the music of the black artists.

The whites took to the blues so rapidly that the major record companies decided to expand their record buying public to include white distributors and jobbers to stock the records in white stores. To accomplish this, they had to change the term 'race' records to rhythm and blues. This transformation took place in 1949. When rhythm and blues (R&B) was officially adopted in 1949, many disc jockeys, music critics and record companies thought that that was the end of the blues. Rhythm and blues was not a racial euphemism that applied to only one group of people. Unlike 'race' records that have been in existence since 1920 and included all types of black music, such as, jazz, blues, gospels, spirituals, string bands, washboard and jug bands and standard pop music primarily targeted for the black public, R&B embraced both the blacks and whites.

During the decade of the 1950s, there were some black artists that expressed their dislike for the blues. One such person was Ruth Brown. But after some professional guidance from Blanche Calloway, Cab Calloway's sister and Atlantic Records executives, Ruth changed her tune about the blues and eventually became regarded as 'Queen Mother of the Blues."

The blues however, did take a decline in popularity during the 1950s and blues musicians and songsters found places to perform hard to come by and therefore many of them had to find daytime jobs to make ends meet. Guitarist Nehemiah 'Skip' James had to return to Mississippi to work on the farm as a sharecropper, Eddie 'Son' House at one time was considered one of the best blues musician and singer was forced to put away his guitar to work for the railroad company as a porter and a barbecue chef. Gus Cannon and Walter 'Furry' Lewis found employment with the Memphis Sanitation Department as street cleaners. They were pushing brooms on Beale Street in front of the same nightclubs they used to perform in.

In 1960, Willie Dixon and Memphis Slim decided to bring new life into the fading blues by leaving Chicago for a European tour. Their performances throughout Europe proved to be successful that the blues became alive again in the United States. The blues have recaptured the hearts of the blacks and a new breed of white audiences. Nightclubs were opening up for the blues artists in Chicago, Detroit, Memphis, New York and many southern cities along the Mississippi Delta. The American Folk Blues Festivals made an extensive tour throughout Europe and the United States. During the next three decades new blues artists were being discovered.

Etta James, born on January 25, 1938 in Los Angeles emulated two great ladies that sang the blues long before she was born. They were, 'Ma' Rainey and Bessie Smith. Etta's blues renditions were always expressed with deep emotions. Her up-tempo blues could be as explosive as Memphis Minnie McCoy or Lucille Bogan. Etta's success did not come easy. Although she had several hits on the rhythm and blues charts, such as, "The Wallflower," "All I Could Do Was Cry," "Something's Got a Hold of Me," "Stop the Wedding" and "Tell Mama." They did not fully express her inner feelings as only the blues could do. 1970 was a bad decade for her. She had no recording contract. She was not able to get bookings in the bigger and better clubs, whereas, she had to take whatever was available, like small clubs, coffee shops and local bars. She lived in a cheap, run-down hotel and was often found roaming the streets at night. Then in 1978, the Rolling Stones heard of her and used Etta as their opening act. Etta James never looked back. She won a Grammy for the best jazz performance for "Mystery Lady." She was inducted into the Rock and Roll Hall of Fame. She has won phrases from many prominent people in the music industry; "One of the great forces in American music," "One of the greatest vocalists since Billie Holiday," and "The greatest of all modern blues singers, the undisputed earth mother." Her focus is straight ahead and is often referred to today as the "Queen of the Blues."

Albert Collins made his debut on the blues scene in 1958 with the first single release of "The Freeze" on a 45RPM record. After receiving recognition from his single success, he was invited to join Little Richard's band, replacing Jimi Hendrix. Collins is known for his fast powerful guitar playing that always generates a foot stomping audience. Collins credits his love for the blues with his close associations with his cousin Sam 'Lightnin' Hopkins. T-Bone Walker, Gatemouth Brown and B.B. King. During the 1960s and 1970s he was constantly on tours with various groups and recording for Imperial Records. In the 1980s, he became the number one recording artist for Alligator Records, winning awards and Grammy's from around the world. Unfortunately, during the midst of his deserved fame he died of cancer on November 24, 1993.

Robert Cray was born in Columbus, Georgia in 1953, and by the time he was 13 years old, he got his first guitar and joined a local band for experience. Robert was influenced with the guitar style of Albert Collins. In 1978, he recorded his first album for Tomato Records title, "Who's Been Talking." In 1983, he recorded "Bad Influence" for High Tone Records that got him nationwide acceptance as a true blues artist. He was able to do that with the sale of more than a million albums of his "Strong Persuader" release. Today, in the 2000s, he is still in constant demand with his videos on MTV regularly and performing to a sell out concert. Many young artists look up to Cray as their role model, a good choice for the youngsters.

Harmonica player Billy Branch began his professional career during the late 1960s while he was still in his young teenage period. Willie Dixon took Billy under his wing and guided him on the proper playing of the harmonica. It didn't take Billy long to get into a blues group with pianist Jimmy Walker. Branch made his first record with the Barrelhouse Label "Bring Me another Half a Pint" and then moved on to Alligator Records with "Living Chicago Blues." With his band the Sons of Blues, they are constantly on tour, and through the Urban Gateways Organization, Billy provides live blues music and a discussion of the blues to Chicago's school students.

These are just a few of today's outstanding blues performers. Recognition however, must be given to C. J. Chenier, Kenny Neal, Vasti Jackson, Barbara Carr, Lurrie Bell, Son Seals, Fenton Robinson, Delbert McClinton, James Cotton, Johnny Copeland and Marva White. The blues is very much alive today-the perpetual flame that never goes out. More concert tours are organized the world over with sell-out attendance. Today's blues artists are transmitting the message of our past idols as Blind Lemon Jefferson, Leadbelly, Muddy Waters, Tampa Red, Big Bill Broonzy, Howlin' Wolf, 'Ma' Rainey, Mamie Smith, Bessie Smith, and Memphis Minnie McCoy.

The more than 160 blues societies throughout the United States, Canada and Europe are constantly keeping the perpetual blues flame alive with their distribution of newsletters to keep their members of which there are more than 100,000 informed of all the latest information about blues artists and concerts.

When the blues emerged from the depth of the Mississippi Delta, it depicted the hardships, sufferings and inhumane treatments of the black people. They were forced to work at hard labor on the plantations, the docks, in chain-gangs and in construction camps. The black women were sexually abused unmercifully. However, as time pressed forward the views, the thinking and the opinions about the blues and its people has changed with the Americans and Europeans. They now embrace the blues unbiased and without prejudice whole heartedly.

ARTISTS	TITLE
Brown, James	Godfather of the Blues
Brown, Ruth	Queen Mother of the Blues
Bunch, William (Peetie Wheatstraw)	The Devil's Son-in-Law / The High Sheriff From Hell
Chapman, Peter (Memphis Slim)	The Ambassador of the Blues
Chenier, Clifton	King of Zydeco Music
Cox, Ida	Uncrowned Queen of the Blues
Dixon, Floyd	Mr. Magnificent
Franklin, Aretha	Queen of Soul
Handy, W.C.	Father of the Blues
Jordan, Louis	Father of Rhythm & Blues
King, B.B.	King of the Blues
Mayfield, Percy	The Poet Laureate of the Blues
Patton, Charley	Founder of the Delta Blues
Rainey, Gertrude 'MA'	Mother of the Blues
Raitt, Bonnie	Daughter of the Blues
Rodgers, Jimmy	Father of 'Hillbilly' or Country and Western Music
Smith, Bessie	Empress of the Blues
Smith, Clara	World's Champion Moaner
Stokes, Frank	King of Beale Street
Taylor, KoKo	Queen of the Blues
Turner, Joseph (Big Joe)	The Singing Bartender

NAME	BIRTHPLACE	BORN	DIED
Alexander, Alger ('Texas')	Texas	1900	1954
Allen, Fulton (Blind Boy Fuller)	North Carolina	1909	1941
Allison, Luther	Arkansas	1939	1997
Ammons, Albert	Illinois	1907	1949
Armstrong, Louis	Louisiana	1900	1971
Arnold, James ('Kokomo')	Georgia	1901	1968
Arnold, William (Billy Boy Arnold)	Illinois	1935	
Banjo Joe (Gus Cannon)	Mississippi	1883	1979
Basie, Count	New Jersey	1904	1984
Barbecue Bob (Robert Hicks)	Georgia	1902	1931
Below, Fred	Illinois	1926	1988
Benton, Buster	Arkansas	1932	1996
'Big Bill' Broonzy (William Lee Conley)	Mississippi	1893	1958
'Big Joe' Turner (Joseph Vernon Turner)	Missouri	1911	1985
Blackwell, Francis 'Scrapper'	Indiana	1906	1962
Blake, Arthur (Blind Blake)	Florida	1895	1935
Blakemore, Amos Wells (Junior Wells)	Arkansas	1934	1998
Bland, Bobby 'Blue' (Robert Calvin)	Tennessee	1930	
Bloomfield, Mike	Illinois	1943	1981
Bogan, Lucille (Bessie Jackson)	Mississippi	1897	1948
Boogie Man (John Lee Hooker)	Mississippi	1920	2001
Booker, John Lee (John Lee Hooker)	Mississippi	1920	2001
Boyd, Eddie	Mississippi	1914	1994
Branch, Billy	Illinois	1951	
Brown, Charles	Texas	1922	

Brown, Clarence 'Gatemouth'	Louisiana	1924	
Brown, James	Tennessee	1928	
Brown, Robert (Washboard Sam)	Illinois	1906	1966
Brown, Roy	Louisiana	1925	1981
Brown, Ruth (Ruth Weston)	Virginia	1928	
Bumble Bee Slim (Amos Easton)	Georgia	1905	1968
Bunch, William (Peetie Wheatstraw)	Tennessee	1902	1941
Burnett, Chester (Howlin' Wolf)	Mississippi	1910	1976
Butterfield, Paul	Illinois	1941	1988
Calvin, Robert (Bobby 'Blue' Bland)	Tennessee	1930	
Cannon, Gus (Banjo Joe)	Mississippi	1883	1979
Carr, Leroy	Tennessee	1905	1935
Carter, Bo (Armenter Chapmon)	Mississippi	1893	1964
Chapman, Peter (Memphis Slim)	Mississippi	1915	1988
Charles, Ray	Georgia	1932	
Chapmon, Armentor (Bo Carter)	Mississippi	1893	1964
Chenier, Clifton	Louisiana	1925	1987
Chenier, C.J.	Texas	1957	
Collins, Albert	Texas	1932	1993
Conley, William Lee ('Big Bill' Broonzy)	Mississippi	1893	1958
Copeland, James	Texas	1937	
Copeland, Johnny	Louisiana	1937	
Cotton, James	Mississippi	1935	
Cox, Ida	Georgia	1896	1967
Cray, Robert	Georgia	1953	
Crayton, PeeWee	Texas	1914	1985
Crudup, Arthur 'Big Boy'	Mississippi	1905	1974

Davenport, Charles 'Cow Cow'	Alabama	1894	1955
Davis, Gary 'Blind'	South Carolina	1896	1972
Davis, Walter	North Carolina	1912	1964
Dawkins, Jimmy	Mississippi	1936	
Dixon, Willie	Mississippi	1915	1992
Dorsey, Thomas A. (Georgia Tom)	Georgia	1899	1993
Douglas, K.C.	Mississippi	1913	1975
Douglas, Minnie (Memphis Minnie McCoy)	Louisiana	1896	1973
DuPree, Champion Jack	Louisiana	1910	1992
Eaglin, Snooks	Louisiana	1936	
Estes, John Adams ('Sleepy John')	Tennessee	1899	1977
Floyd, Frank 'Harmonica'	Mississippi	1908	1984
Franklin, Aretha	Michigan	1942	
Fuller, Allen (Blind Boy Fuller)	North Carolina	1909	1941
Fuller, Jesse	California	1896	1975
Fulson, Lowell	Oklahoma	1921	1999
Georgia Tom (Thomas A. Dorsey)	Georgia	1899	1993
Gillum, William (Jazz Gillum)	Mississippi	1904	1964
Green, Lil	Mississippi	1919	1954
Guy, George 'Buddy'	Louisiana	1936	
Hadley, Elder J.J. (Charley Patton)	Mississippi	1887	1934
Handy, William C.	Alabama	1873	1958
Harris, Wynonie	Nebraska	1920	1969
Hemphill, Jesse Mae	Mississippi	1934	
Henderson, Fletcher	Georgia	1897	1952
Henderson, Rosa	Kentucky	1896	1968
Hicks, Robert (Barbecue Bob)	Georgia	1902	1931

Hill, Bertha 'Chippie	South Catolina	1905	1950
Hill, Z.Z.	Texas	1941	1984
Holiday, Billie	Maryland	1915	1959
Hooker, John Lee	Mississippi	1920	2001
Hopkins, Sam 'Lightin'	Texas	1912	1982
Horton, Walter 'Shakey'	Mississippi	1917	1981
House, Eddie 'Son'	Mississippi	1902	1988
Howell, Joshua Barnes ('Peg Leg')	Georgia	1888	1966
Howlin' Wolf (Chester Burnett)	Mississippi	1910	1976
Hunter, Alberta	Tennessee	1895	1984
Hurt, John	Mississippi	1894	1966
Jackson, Bessie (Lucille Bogan)	Mississippi	1897	1948
Jackson, Jim	Mississippi	1880	1938
Jackson, John	Washington, D.C.	1924	2002
Jackson, CHarlie 'Papa'	Louisiana	1885	1935
Jackson, Vasti	Mississippi	1959	
Jacobs, 'Little Walter'	Louisiana	1930	1968
James, Elmore	Mississippi	1918	1963
James, Etta	California	1938	
James, Nehemiah 'Skip'	Mississippi	1902	1969
Jazz Gillum (William Gillum)	Mississippi	1904	1964
Jefferson, Blind Lemon	Texas	1897	1930
Johnson, Alonzo 'Lonnie'	Louisiana	1889	1970
Johnson, Jimmie	Mississippi	1928	
Johnson, Johnnie	West Virginia	1924	
Johnson, Robert	Mississippi	1912	1938
Johnson, Tommy	Mississippi	1896	1956
Jones, Curtis	Texas	1906	1973
King, Albert	Mississippi	1924	1993
King, B.B.	Mississippi	1925	
King, Freddy	Texas	1934	1976

Name	State	Born	Died
Lane, James A. (Jimmy Rogers)	Mississippi	1897	1933
Leadbelly (Huddie Ledbetter)	Louisiana	1885	1949
Ledbetter, Huddie (Leadbelly)	Louisiana	1885	1949
Lee, Johnny (John Lee Hooker)	Mississippi	1920	2001
Lenoir, J.B.	Illinois	1929	1967
Lewis, Walter 'Furry'	Mississippi	1893	1981
Liggins, Joe	Oklahoma	1916	1987
Lipscomb, Mance	Texas	1895	1976
Little Brother Montgomery (Eurreal Wilford Mongomery)	Louisiana	1906	1984
Littlejohn, Johnny	Mississippi	1931	1994
Little Walter	Louisiana	1930	1968
Lockwood, Robert	Arkansas	1915	
Lofton, Clarence 'Cripple'	Tennessee	1887	1957
Luandrew, Albert (Sunnyland Slim)	Mississippi	1907	1995
Maghett, Sam 'Magic Sam'	Illinois	1937	1969
Mayfield, Percy	Louisiana	1920	1984
McClennan, Tommy	Mississippi	1908	1962
McClinton, Delbert	Texas	1940	
McCollum, Robert (Robert Noghthawk)	Illinois	1919	1967
McCoy, Memphis Minnie (Minnie Douglas)	Louisiana	1896	1973
McDowell, Fred	Mississippi	1905	1972
McTell, Willie Blind	Georgia	1898	1959
Memphis Slim (Peter Chapman)	Mississippi	1915	1988
Merriweather, Major ('Big Maceo')	Georgia	1905	1953
Montgomery, Eurreal Wilford ('Little Brother')	Louisiana	1906	1984
Morganfield, McKinley (Muddy Waters)	Mississippi	1915	1983

Morton, Jelly Roll	Louisiana	1890	1941
Moss, Buddy	Georgia	1914	1984
Muddy Waters (McKinley Morganfield)	Mississippi	1915	1983
Musselwhite, Charlie	Mississippi	1944	
Neal, Kenny	Louisiana	1957	
Nighthawk, Robert (Robert McCollum)	Illinois	1919	1967
Parker, 'Little Junior'	Tennessee	1932	1971
Patton, Charley	Mississippi	1887	1934
Pridgett, Gertrude (Gertrude 'MA' Rainey)	Georgia	1886	1939
Pryor, Snooky	Mississippi	1921	
Rachel, Yank	Tennessee	1910	1997
Rainey, Gertrude 'MA' (Gertrude Pridgett)	Georgia	1886	1939
Reed, Jimmy	Mississippi	1925	1976
Robinson, Fenton	Mississippi	1935	1997
Rodgers, Jimmy	Mississippi	1897	1933
Rogers, Jimmy (James A. Lane)	Mississippi		
Rush, Otis	Mississippi	1934	
Rushing, Jimmy	Oklahoma	1903	1972
Sam, Birmingham (John Lee Hooker)	Mississippi	1920	2001
Seals, Son	Arkansas	1942	
Shines, Johnny	Tennessee	1915	1992
Sims, Frankie Lee	Texas	1917	1970
Sister Rosetta Tharpe	Arkansas	1915	1973
'Sleepy John Estes' (John Adams Estes)	Tennessee	1899	1977
Slim, Texas (John Lee Hooker)	Mississippi	1920	2001
Smith, Bessie	Tennessee	1894	1937
Smith, Clara	South Carolina	1894	1935
Smith, Clarence 'Pinetop'	Alabama	1904	1929
Smith, Mamie	Ohio	1883	1946
Smith, Trixie	Georgia	1895	1943

Spann, Otis	Mississippi	1931	1970
Spivey, Victoria	Texas	1906	1976
Stokes, Frank	Mississippi	1883	1954
Sumlin, Hubert	Mississippi	1931	
Sykes, Roosevelt	Arkansas	1906	1983
Taj Mahal	Massachuetts	1942	
Tampa Red (Hudson Whittaker)	Florida	1903	1981
Taylor, Arthur 'Montana'	Indiana	1903	1954
Taylor, Eddie	Mississippi	1923	1985
Taylor, KoKo (Cora Walton)	Tennessee	1935	
T-Bone Walker (Aaron Thibeaux)	Texas	1910	1975
Terrell, Sanders (Sonny Terrell)	Georgia	1911	1986
Tharpe, Rosetta Sister	Arkansas	1915	1973
Thibeaux, Aaron (T-Bone Walker)	Texas	1910	1975
Thomas, Henry	Texas	1874	1959
Thomas, Hociel	Texas	1904	1952
Thomas, Rufus	Tennessee	1917	
Thornton, Willie Mae ('Big Mama'(	Texas	1926	1984
Townsend, Henry	MIchigan	1909	
Turner, Joseph Vernon ('Big Joe' Turner)	Missouri	1911	1985
Vaughan, Sarah	New Jersey	1924	1990
Vinson, Eddie (Mister Cleanhead)	Texas	1917	1988
Wallace, Beulah 'Sippie'	Texas	1898	1986
Walter, Little	Louisiana	1930	1968
Walton, Cora (KoKo Taylor)	Tennessee	1935	
Washboard Sam (Robert Brown)	Illinois	1906	1966
Watson, Johnny (Daddy Stove Pipe)	Texas	1935	1996

Weldon, 'Casey Bill'	Arkansas	1909	
Wells, Junior (Amos Wells Blakemore)	Tennessee	1932	1998
Wheatstraw, Peetie (William Bunch)	Tennessee	1902	1941
White, Booker T. Washington (Bukka White)	Mississippi	1909	1977
White, Georgia		1903	1980
White, Joshua Daniel 'Josh'	South Carolina	1915	1969
White, Lynn	Alabama	1953	
Whittaker, Hudson (Tampa Red)	Florida	1903	1981
Williams, 'Big Joe'	Mississippi	1903	1982
Williams, Johnny (John Lee Hooker)	Mississippi	1920	2001
Williams, Robert Pete	Louisiana	1941	1980
Williamson, Aleck ('Rice' Miller)	Mississippi	1897	1965
Williamson, John Lee	Tennessee	1916	1948
Woods, Oscar 'Buddy'	Louisiana	1890	1950
Yancey, Jimmy	Illinois	1898	1951
Young, Mighty Joe	Louisiana	1927	

BIBLIOGRAPHY

Awmiller, Craig. This House On Fire. New York: Franklin Watts, 1996

Bane, Michael. White Boy Singin' The Blues. New York: Da Capo Press, 1992

Berkow, Ira. Maxwell Street. New York: Doubleday & Company, 1977

Campbell, Michael. And The Beat Goes On. New York: Schirmer Books, 1996

Cohn, Lawrence. Nothing But The Blues. New York: Abbeville Press, 1993

Davis, Francis. The History Of The Blues. New York: Hyperion, 1995

Dickerson, James. Goin' Back To Memphis. New York: Schirmer Books, 1996

Lomax, Alan. The Land Where The Blues Began. New York: Pantheon Books, 1993

Oliver, Paul. The New Grove Gospel, Blues and Jazz. New York: W.W.Norton & Company, 1986

Schuller, Gunther. Early Jazz. New York" Oxford University Press, 1968

Shaw, Arnold. Honkers and Shouters. New York: Collier Books, 1978

Taylor, Marc. A Touch of Classic Soul. New York: Aloiv Publishing Co. 1996

Blues Societies & Organizations

Alabama

Magic City Blues Society
Contact:Scott Fuller
P.O. Box 360471
Birmingham, AL. 35236
(205) 933-6904
(205) 871-7337 fax

Big Wills Arts Council
Contact: Russell Gulley
200 Gault Ave. S.
Fort Payne, AL. 35967
(205) 845-9591

Alabama Blues Society
Contact: Louise Turner
P.O. Box 20513
Tuscaloosa, AL. 35402
(205) 345-1876

Arizona

Phoenix Blues Society
Contact: Bill Mitchell
P.O. Box 38674
Phoenix, AZ. 85067
(602) 252-0599

Tucson Blues Society
Contact: Pat Desmond
P.O. Box 30672
Tucson, AZ. 85751
(520) 570-7955

Arkansas

Sonny Boy Blues Society
Contact: Houston Stackhouse, Jr.
        Bubba Sullivan
P.O. Box 237
Helena, AR. 72342
(501) 338-3501

Arkansas River Blues Society
P.O. Box 1594
Little Rock, AR. 72203

White River Delta Blues Society
Contact: Dr. David Gray
1005 McLain
Newport, AR. 72112
(501) 523-6365
(501) 523-6984 fax

California

Southern California Blues Society
Contact: Alan Brown
13337 E. South St. Ste. 249
Cerritos, CA. 90703
(310) 495-3424

Central California Blues Society
Contact: Warren Milton
1903 Cedar
Fresno, CA. 93702
(209) 486-8948

Blues Heaven Foundation
Contact: Shirli Dixon Nelson
249 N. Brand Blvd. #590
Glendale, CA. 91203
(818) 507-7613

**International Blues Society
and Percy Mayfield Memorial
Scholarship Fund**
Contact: Tina Mayfield
P.O. Box 82053
Los Angeles, CA. 90037
(805) 267-0495

Mendocino County Blues Society
Contact: Rick Blaufeld
P.O. Box 1144
Mendocino, CA. 95460
(707) 937-5741
(707) 895-3241

Siskiyou Blues Society
Contact: Victor Martin
Keith Anderson
P.O. Box 271
Mt. Shasta, CA. 96067
(916) 926-5823
(916) 938-4739 fax

Bay Area Blues Society
Contact: Ronnie Stewart
408 13th St. Ste. 512
Oakland, CA. 94612
(510) 836-2227
(510) 836-4341 fax

Shasta Blues Society
Contact: Steve Brandon
P.O. Box 994693
Redding, CA. 96099
(916) 378-1980

Sacramento Blues Society
Contact: David Marquez
P.O. Box 60580
Sacramento, CA. 95860
(916) 556-5007

Big Joe Turner Musicians' Fund
Contact: Betty Miller
9000 Fairview Ave. Ste.102
San Gabriel, CA. 91775
(626) 286-2830
Financianl & promotional
assistance for musicians

San Luis Obispo Blues Society
Contact: Bob Oberg
P.O. Box 14041
San Luis Obispo, CA. 93406
(805) 541-7930

Blue Monday Foundation
Contact: Mark Naftalin
116 Du Bois St.
San Rafael, CA. 94901-
(415) 453-7712

Monterey Bay Blues Society
P.O. Box 423
Santa Cruz, CA. 95061

Sonoma County Blues Society
Contact: Cari Chenkin
P.O. Box 7844
Santa Rosa, CA. 94507
(707) 547-9003

North Bay Blues Society
Contact: Darwin Ali
Alvin Ali
P.O. Box 5451
Vallejo, CA. 94591
(707) 552-4271

Colorado

Colorado Blues Society
Contact: David McIntyre
P.O. Box 130
Lyons, CO. 80540
(303) 823-9272

Connecticut

R & B Rock 'n' Roll Society, INC.
Contact: Bill NOlan
P.O. Box 1949
New Haven, CT. 06510
(203) 924-1079

District of Columbia

D.C. Blues Society
Contact: Bob Gray
P.O. Box 77315
Washington, D.C. 20013
(202) 828-3028
(703) 536-0284

Rhythm and Blues Foundation
Contact: Suzan Jenkins
1555 Connecticut Ave. NW, Ste 401
Washington, D.C. 20036
(202) 588-5566
(202) 588-5549 fax

Smithsonian/Folkways
955 L'Enfant Plaza, Ste. 2600
Washington, D.C. 20560
(202) 287-3251
(202) 287-3699 fax

Florida

Orlando Blues Society
Contact: Jim Manuel
608 S. Lake Ave.
Orlando, FL. 32801
(407) 422-8826
(407) 896-6929 fax

Florida Blues Network
Contact: Jerry Ross
6489 Kahoma Way
Sarasota, FL. 34241
(813) 377-8220

Gulf Coast Blues Society
Contact: Gene Hardage
P.O. Box 13513
St. Petersburg, FL. 33733
(813) 822-6615

Big Bend Blues Society
Contact: Alan Rollins
3239 Yorktown Dr.
Tallahassee, FL. 32314
(904) 386-8504

Georgia

Atlanta Blues Preservation Society
Contact: J.J. Holtzman
354 Elmira
Atlanta, GA. 30307
(404) 523-2583

Hawaii

Hawaiian Blues Society
Contact: Rick Spachner
P.O. Box 5497
Kailua-Kona, HI. 96745
(808) 324-6302

East Hawaii Blues Association
Contact: Norman Moody
P.O. Box1221
Kurtistown, HI. 96760
(808) 968-8442

Maui Blues Association
Contact: Lou Wolfenson
P.O. Box 1211
Puunene, HI. 96784
(808) 242-7318
(808) 572-9896 fax

Idaho

Boise Blues Society
Contact: Greg Harley
P.O. Box 2756
Boise, ID. 83701
(208) 344- 2583

Illinois

Center for Black Music Research
Columbia College
600 S. Michigan Ave.
Chicago, IL. 60605
(312) 663-1600 ext.560

Chicago Blues Archives
Contact: Richard Schwegel
Harold Washington Library Center
400 S. State St.
Chicago, IL. 60605
(312) 747-4850

Chicago Blues Society
Contact: Skip Landt
909 W. Armitage Ave.
Chicago, IL. 60614

Foundation for the Advancement
of the Blues
P.O. Box 578486
Chicago, IL. 60657
(312) 278-1352
(312) 278-2773 fax

Rail City Blues Society
P.O. Box 787
Galesburg, IL. 61401

Crossroads Blues Society
Contact: Craig Long
          Liz Sarber
420 W. Locust St.
Lanark, IL. 61046
(815) 493-2241

River City Blues Society
P.O. Box 463
Peoria, IL. 61651

Mid-Mississippi Muddy Water
Blues Society
P.O. Box 887
Quincy, IL. 62306

Illinois Central Blues Club
Contact: Steve Truesdale
P.O. Box 603
Springfield, IL. 62705
(217) 744-3256

Indiana

Blues Society of Indiana
Contact: Tom Coombs
P.O. Box 2263
Indianapolis, IN. 46205
(317) 470-8795

South Bend Blues Society
P.O. Box 8
Notre Dame, IN. 46556
(219) 239-3960

Iowa

Burlington's Great River
Blues Society
Contact: Michael Mayors Entertainment
Box 1134
Burlington, IA. 52601
(319) 753-2982

Mississippi Valley Blues Society
Contact: Joe Griffen
318 Brady St.
Davenport, IA. 52801
(319) 322-5837
(319) 322-3039

Central Iowa Blues Society
Contact: Jeff Wagner
P.O. Box 13016
Des Moines, IA. 50310
(515) 276-0677

Johnson County Blues Society
Contact: Ranko Vujoesvic
P.O. Box 2114
Iowa City, IA. 52244
(319) 335-3364

South Skunk Blues Society
Contact: Jeff Hart
          Junella Yodor
415 W. 12th St.
Newton, IA. 50208
(515) 259-3337
(515) 791-7473

Kansas

Western Kansas Blues Society
Contact: Mike Wisler
322 11th St.
Garden City, KS. 67846
(316) 276-2015

Wichita Blues Society
Contact: Randy Crump
P.O. Box 8273, Munger Stn.
Wichita, KS. 67208
(316) 265-9646

Kentucky

Kyana Blues Society
Contact: Keith Clements
P.O. Box 755
Louisville, KY. 40201
(502) 451-6872
(502) 584-2820 fax

**National Association of
Rhythm and Blues Dee Jay's, Inc.**
Contact: Ron Wallace
1715 Belmar Dr.
Louisville, KY. 40213
(502) 459-4970

Louisiana

**Freelance/Musicians' Association/
Jewish Entertainment Resources**
Contact: Judy Caplan Ginsburgh
P.O. Box 12692
Alexandria, LA. 71315
(318) 442-8863
(318) 443-8816 fax

Louisiana Blues Society
Tabby's Blues Box and
Heritage Hall
1314 North Blvd.
Baton Rouge, LA. 70802

Louisiana Showcase
Contact: Robert M. Calhoun
4606 Jones Creek Rd. Ste. 290
Baton Rouge, LA. 70817
(504) 272-5859
(504) 364-8828

Blues in the Schools
333 St. Charles Ave. Ste. 614
New Orleans, LA. 70130
(504) 522-5533
(504) 522-1159 fax

**Coalition to Preserve the Art
of Street Entertainment**
Contact: Jose Torres Tama
1427 Dauphine St.
New Orleans, LA. 70116
(504) 948-4607

Crescent City Blues Club
333 St. Charles Ave. Ste. 614
New Orleans, LA. 70130
(504) 522-5533

**International House of Blues
Foundation**
Contact: Michelle Rousseau
225 Decatur St.
New Orleans, LA. 70130
(504) 949-7050
(504) 524-4755

New Orleans Blues Society
Contact: Thorny Penfield
1463 Moss St.
New Orleans, LA. 70119
(504) 488-5419

**New Orleans Center for the
Creative Arts (NOCCA)**
Contact: John Otis
6048 Perrier St.
New Orleans, LA. 70118
(504) 899-0055

**New Orleans Jazz and Heritage
Foundation, Inc.**
1205 N. Rampart St.
New Orleans, LA. 70116
(504) 422-4786
(504) 522-5456

Young Leadership Council
Music Link Committee
Contact: Ann McAdams
333 St. Charles Ave. Ste.1402
New Orleans, LA. 70130-3167
(504) 582-1218

Maine

Southern Maine Blues Society
Contact: Sharon Hooper
P.O. Box 4703
Portland, ME. 04112

Maryland

Baltimore Blues Society, Inc.
Contact Dale Patton
P.O. Box 26250
Baltimore, MD. 21210
(410) 329-5825
(410) 771-4862 fax

Massachusetts

Boston Blues Society
P.O. Box 850-345
Braintree, MA. 02185
(617) 843-5403

Michigan

Mid-Michigan Blues Society
2756 E. Grand River Ave. Lot A-18
East Lansing, MI. 48823

West Michigan Blues Society
Contact: Jimmie Stagger
P.O. Box 6985
Grand Rapids, MI. 49516
(616) 456-1871
(616) 458-1011 fax

Capital Area Blues Society
Contact: Bonnie Stebbins
P.O. Box 1004
Okemos, MI. 48805
(517) 349-0006
(517) 349-4731

Mississippi

Delta Blues Education Fund
Contact: John Ruskey
291 Sunflower Ave.
Clarksdale, MS. 38614
(601) 627-4070
(601) 627-7263 fax

Delta Blues Museum
Contact: Ron Gorsegner
114 Delta Ave.
Clarksdale, MS. 38614
(601) 627-6820
(601) 627-4344 fax

Sunflower River Blues Association
Contact: Jim & Selina O'Neal
P.O. Box 1562
Clarksdale, MS. 38614
(601) 627-6820

Blues Archive
Contact: Edwaed Komara
Farley Hall, University of
Mississippi
University, MS. 38677
(601) 232-7753
(601) 232-5161 fax

Missouri

Kansas City Blues Society
Contact: Shirley Mae Owens
P.O. Box 32131
Kansas City, MO. 64171
(816) 737-0713
(816) 889-3832 fax

Missouri Musical Heritage
Foundation
Box 21652
St. Louis, MO. 63109
(314) 647-2447
(314) 647-2497 fax

St. Louis Blues Society
Contact: John May
P.O. Box 78894
St. Louis, MO. 63178
(314) 241-2583

MONTANA

Billings Blues and Jazz Society
3917 Lauredo PL.
Billings, MT. 59106

Bozeman Blues and Jazz Society
702 S. 7th St.
Bozeman, MT. 59715

Helena Blues and Jazz Society
Box 992
Helena, MT. 59624

Missoula Blues and Jazz Society
Contact: Bruce Micklus
237 Blaine St.
Missoula, MT. 59801
(406) 542-0077

Nevada

Las Vegas Blues Society
Contact: Bill Cherry
P.O. Box 27871
Las Vegas, NV. 89126
(702) 251-9398
(702) 253-5252 hotline

Music Society of the Americas
Contact: John Earl Williams
906 Dale St.
Las Vegas, NV. 89108
(702) 646-4865
(702) 648-5135 fax

New Jersey

Blues Power Blues Society
Contact: Sharon Roberts
44 Telford St.
East Orange, N.J. 07018
(201) 675-3276
(201) 675-3276 fax

Skylands Blues Society
Contact: Scott Acton
P.O. Box 857
Hackettstown, N.J. 07840
(908) 813-2587
(908) 850-5102

New York

Blues Society of Western New York
P.O. Box 129, Kenmore Branch
Buffalo, N.Y. 14217

Lead Belly Society
P.O. Box 6679
Ithaca, N.Y. 14851
(607) 273-6615
(607) 844-4810

Manhattan Blues Alliance Plus
Towne Terrace, Ste. 16A
Middletown, N.Y. 10940
(914) 346-4613

Archive of Contemporary Music
Contact: B. George
54 White St.
New York, N.Y. 10013
(212) 226-6967
(212) 226-6540 fax

Blues Connection of Central New York
Contact: Kim Ahern
121 Everingham Rd.
Syracuse, N.Y. 13205-3234
(315) 469-5821
(315) 469-6257 fax

North Carolina

Charlotte Blues Society
Contact: Beth Pollhammer
P.O. Box 172, Elizabeth Contact Sta.
Charlotte, N.C. 28204
(704) 455-5875
(704) 331-8871
(704) 455-6065 fax

Piedmont Blues Preservation Society
Contact: John Amberg
P.O. Box 9737
Greensboro, N.C. 27429
(910) 333-1994
(910) 274-5745

Music Maker Relief Foundation
Contact: Timothy Duffy
Rt. 1, Box 567
Pinnacle, N.C. 27043
(910) 325-3261
(910) 325-3263

Blues Society of the Lower Cape Fear
P.O. Box 1487
Wilmington, N.C. 28402

Ohio

Greater Cincinnatti Blues Society
Contact: Kitty Carson
P.O. Box 6028
Cincinnatti, OH. 45206
(513) 721-0314

Columbus Blues Alliance
Contact: Sean H. Carney
        Jim Biersdorf
P.O. Box 82451
Columbus, OH. 43202
(614) 470-2222

Blues, Jazz and Folk Music Society
P.O. Box 2122
Marietta, OH. 45750
(614) 373-6640

Oklahoma

Oklahoma Blues Society
Contact: Jenny Oblander
P.O. Box 76176
Oklahoma City, OK. 73147-2176
(405) 791-0110

Tulsa Blues Club
Contact: Jeanie Webster
         Curt Abbott
P.O. Box 702426
Tulsa, OK. 74170-2426
(918) 436-8774
(918) 252-0049

Oregon

Cascade Blues Association
Contact: Erroll Shervey
P.O. Box 14493
Portland, OR. 97214
(503) 233-7470

Pennsylvania

Lehigh Valley Blues Network
Contact: Jim Mertz
517 N. 6th St.
Allentown, PA. 18102
(610) 437-3217

The Blues Group
Contact: Amy Saslaff
P.O. Box 674
Bangor, PA. 18013
(215) 588-4158

Mon-Valley Blues Society
Contact: Wilbur Landman
P.O. Box 155
Hibbs, PA. 15443

Billtown Blues Association, Inc.
Contact: Bonnie Tallman
P.O. Box 2
Hughesville, PA. 17737
(717) 584-4298

Bessie Smith Society
Contact: Michael Roth
Franklin and Marshall College
Lancaster, PA. 17603
(717) 291-3915

Bucks County Blues Society
Contact: Thomas J. Cullen
P.O. Box 482
Levittown, PA. 19058
(215) 946-4794

Philadelphia Blues Machine
Contact: Doug Waltnor
351 Pelham Rd.
Philadelphia, PA. 19119
(215) 849-5465

St. Benedict Blues Society
Contact: Al Alavinski
P.O. Box 104
St. Benedict, PA. 15773-0104

South Carolina

Lowcountry Blues Society
Contact: Gary Erwin
P.O. Box 291
Mt. Pleasant, S.C. 29464
(803) 722-3263
(803) 762-9124 fax

Tennessee

Beale Street Blues Society
Contact: Paul Averwater
P.O. Box 3421
Memphis, TN. 38103
(901) 458-7151

The Blues Foundation
49 Union Ave.
Memphis, TN. 38103
(901) 527-2583
(901) 529-4030 fax

Center for Southern Folklore
Contact: Judy Peiser
130 Beale St.
Memphis, TN. 38103
(901) 525-3655
(901) 525-3945

Music City Blues Society
Contact: Nigel Paul
P.O. Box 22852
Nashville, TN. 37202
(615) 885-4684
(615) 331-0889 fax

Bessie Smith Hall
d/o Dr. Russell J. Linnemann
4342 Comet Trail
Nixson, TN. 37343

Texas

Dallas Blues Society
P.O. Box 190406
Dallas, TX. 75219

Stevie Ray Vaughan Fan Club
Contact: Lee Hopkins
P.O. Box 800353
Dallas, TX. 75380
(214) 661-2604

Houston Blues Society
Contact: Sonny Boy Terry
P.O. Box 7809
Houston, TX. 77270-7809
(713) 869-7746

Virginia

James River Blues Society
Contact: Jan Ramsey
P.O. Box 4064
Lynchburg, VA. 24502
(804) 239-3042

Natchol' Blues Network, Inc.
Contact: Cathy Dixson
　　　　　Mark Johnson
P.O. Box 1773
Norfolk, VA. 23501-1773
(804) 456-1675
(804) 481-9254
(804) 481-0762 fax

Washington

Washington Blues Society
Contact: Rod Downing
P.O. Box 12215
Seattle, WA. 98102
(206) 783-8389
(206) 783-1475

Walla Walla Blues Society
P.O. Box 906
Walla Walla, Wa. 99362
(509) 525-4240

Wisconsin

Madison Blues
Contact: Gretchen Reinke
P.O. Box 3202
Madison, WI. 53704-0202
(608) 249-0594

Milwaukee Blues Unlimited
Contact: Jim Feeney
4133 N. Bartlett Ave.
Milwaukie, WI. 53211
(414) 964-3693
(414) 647-1725

Wisconsin Blues Society
Contact: Tom Radai
2613 S. 51st St.
Milwaukee, WI. 53219
(414) 321-0188
(608) 362-3969

Canada

Coastal Jazz and Blues Society
Contact: John Orysik
435 W. Hastings St.
Vancouver, BC. Canada V6B 1L4
(604) 682-0706
(604) 682-0704 fax

Hamilton Blues Society
P.O. Box 3632 5tn. C
Hamilton, Ontario, Canada L8H 7N1

Sudbury Blues Society
Contact: Tony Anselmo
46 Rio Rd.
Sudbury, Ontario, Canada P3C 3A5
(705) 673-9751
(705) 675-8012 fax

Toronto Blues Society
Contact: Barbara Isherwood
544 Richmond St. W.
Toronto, Ontario, Canada M5V 1Y4
(416) 504-2037
(416) 504-2078 fAX

OVERSEAS

Australia

Melbourne Blues Appreciation Society
Contact: Geoff Spiegel
　　　　　Steve Fraser
P.O. Box 1249
St. Kilda South
Victoria, Australia 3182
(613) 9580 5963
(613) 9543 2229

Sydney Blues Society
Contact: Dave Harding
　　　　　Julie Fehberg
C1 P.O. Box 520
Alexandria, NSW 2015 Australia
(02) 6248420
(02) 9673908
(02) 3104757 fax

Austria

Vienna Blues Society
Contact: Hans Thelst
Alster Str. 37/18
Nienna, Austria A-1080

England

British Blues Network
15 Chippenham Rd.
London, England W9 2AH
(071) 289-6394

Southside Blues Society
Contact: Ray Gordon
c/o Glebe Farm House
Small Lane, Earlswood
West Midlands, England B94 5EL

Germany

German Blues Circle
Postfach 180 212
Frankfort 18 D-6000 Germany

Italy

Soul & Jazz Society
P.O. Box n. 1012
40124 Bologno, Italy
+39 51 573032
+39 51 242939 fax

The Netherlands

Dutch Blues and Boogie Organization
Contact: Martin Von Olderen
P.O. Box 12538
1100 AM Amsterdam, Zuidcost
Netherlands
020 6961111

Norway

Sotra Blues Club
Contact: Per C. Aarsand
Steinsvikun 70
5353 Straume, Norway
47 56 331910

Boe Blues Club
Postbaks 153
N-2420 Trysil, Norway

Brygga Bluesklubb
Contact: Jens O. Sunde
Kjopmannsgaten 19
7013 Trondheim, Norway
07 51 8320

Halden Bluesklubb
Boks 549
1751 Halden, NOrway

Hell Blues Club
Contact: Kiell Inge Broadl
P.O. Box 45
7570 Hell, NOrway
47-74806888
47-74806854 fax

Hisasveien Friday Night Blues Club
Contact: Svgin Berntsen
Hisasveien 51, 4500 Mandal, Norway

Horten Bluesclub
Postboks 470
N-3193 Horten, Norway   150

Tramsa Bluesklubb
Contact: Tore P. Thuen
Skagsliv 7
N-9007 Tramsa, Norway

Trondheims Bluesklubb
Postsboks 4556
Kalvskinnet, 7002
Trondheim, Norway

Sweden

Amal's Blues Forening
Contact: Nils Lonnsjo
662 95 Fengersfors, Sweden
0532-23394

Blue Monday
Goverth
Vetterslundsg 18 3 tr
724 62 Vasteros, Sweden
46-31-418182
46-21-418182 fax

Dellenbygdens Bluesforening
Contact: Mats Norin
Olnirsvagen 52c
S-820 60 Delsbo, Sweden
01146-65310963

Haninge Bluesforening
Salhemsv. 23
S-137 40 Vasterhaninge, Sweden

International Blues Society
Kabyssg 80
S-414 60 Gateborg, Sweden

Jarfalla BluesForening
Contact: Bo Majling
Ekedolxv 91
175 39 Jarfalla, Sweden

Jazz and Blues i Alvesta
Contact: Lea Nielsen
Lkarydxv
76 342 34 Alvesta, Sweden

Jazz and Blues i Ronneby
Contact: Goran Erikson
Stenbocksv 13
372 00 Ronneby, Sweden

Kiruna Jazz Och Blues
Contact: Lasse Larson
Hermelinsgatan S
981 39 Kiruna, Sweden

Malmo Blues Association
Contact: Tore Martinsson
Falkenbergsg 6B
214 24 Malmo, Sweden

Scandinavian Blues Association
Contact: Tommy Bjorck
Box 4020
S-102 61 Stockholm, Sweden
+46(0) 87148508
+46(0) 7022118 fax

Scandinavian Blues Society
Contact: Namde Mansgatan
S 725-75V
A'Sreras, Sweden

Sodertalje bluesforening
Contact: Lars Granath
Osterg 10
151 43 Sodertalje, Sweden

Stromsunds Jazz and Bluesklubb
Contact: Lars Berglund
Stramsv 42
833 35 Stromsund, Sweden

Sundsvalls Blues Klubb
Contact: Rolf Sundin
Rebetskyg 248
854 60 Sundsvall, Sweden

Uppsala Bluesforening
Box 2107
S-750 02 Uppsala, Sweden

Switzerland

Natchez Trace's Southern Cross
Blues Society
Contact: Phillip Handrickson
Summergasse 29
Basel CH-4056, Switzerland

INDEX

Ace, Johnny, 29
Ace of Hearts Records 125
Acorn Records, 23
Acuff, Roy, 30, 40, 98
Adins, George, 124
Aladdin Records, 19, 24, 26
Alexander, Alger 'Texas' 41, 97, 137
Alexander, John, 29
Allen, Austin, 95
Allen, Fulton, 137
Allen, Henry 'Red', 17
Allen, Lee, 95
Allen, O.K., 68
Alligator Records, 15, 27, 32, 131-2
Allison, Luther, 119, 137
American Folk Blues Festival, 28, 34, 47-9, 117, 119, 127, 130
American Music Records, 69
Ammons, Albert, 50, 69, 80, 137
Anderson, Ivy, 19
Andrew Sisters, 51
Animals, the, 89, 123, 126
Anka, Paul, 115
Ann Arbor Blues Festival, 49, 87
Anthony, Eddie, 74
Antone Records, 26
Apollo Records, 33
Archoolie Records, 100
Ardoin, Bois-See, 101
Ardoin, Lawrence, 101

Aristocrat Records, 33, 45, 83-4
Armstrong, Louis, 11, 17, 20, 47, 103, 137
Arnold, James 'Kokomo' 41, 55, 98, 122, 137
Arnold, Jerome, 32
Arnold, William, 31-2, 119, 137
Asch Records, 99
Ashford, Hammitt, 71
Atlantic Records, 19, 21, 44, 92, 111, 120, 130
Austin, Lovie, 18
Autry, Gene, 98
Avery, Charles, 79

Babineaux, Sidney, 101
Bailey, Mildred, 19
Bailey, Pearl, 20
Banjo Joe, 62, 137-8
Barbecue Bob, 74, 137, 139
Barber, Chris, 52
Barnes, George, 97
Barnes, Joshua, 122
Barnet, Charlie, 50
Barrelhouse Records, 132
Basie, Count, 19, 43, 50, 112, 121, 137
Beale Street Jug Band, 62
Beale Streeters, 29
Beale Street Sheiks, 37
Beatles, 115, 123
Beatty, Josephine, 20
Bechet, Sidney, 20
Beck, Jeff, 118
Behrens, Jerry, 98
Bell, Lurrie, 132
Below, Fred, 84, 137

Bennett, Buster, 54, 137
Bennett Records, 73
Bentley, Gladys, 97
Bernhardt, Clyde, 19
Berry, Chuck, 24, 26, 30-1, 34, 45, 111, 114, 117-8
'Big Bill' 33
Big Crawford, 26, 83
Big Maceo, 28, 51, 82, 141
Big Town Records, 121
Biharis Brothers, 29
Biharis Records, 29
Biltmore Records, 20
Birmingham Jug Band, 47, 62-3
Birmingham Sam, 23
Bishop, Elvis, 119
Black & Blue, 21
Black Louisiana Jug Band, 63
Blackman, Junior, 32
Blakemore, Amos Wells, 28, 137
Blackwell, Francis 'Scrapper' 41-3, 51, 70, 83, 125, 137
Blackwell, Willie, 69
Blake, Arthur, 39, 73, 137
Blake, Eubie, 20
Bland, Robert Calvin, 28, 30
Bland, Bobby 'Blue', 29-30, 47, 92-3, 112, 117, 137
Blood, Sweat & Tears, 115
Bloomfield, Mike, 119, 137
Bluebird Records, 42, 48, 50, 53-4, 63, 67, 98, 111
Blue Flame Syncopaters, 109

Blue Note 4 Records, 50
Blue Records, 33
Blue Ridge Entertainers, 98
Blues Hall of Fame, 24, 30, 47, 122
Blues Progressions, 102
Blues Scale, 109
Blues Serenaders, 20
Blueville Records, 34
Bogan, Lucille, 7, 9, 18-9, 131, 137, 140
Boggs, Dock, 40
Bolden, Buddy, 109
Boogie Man, 23, 137
Booker, John Lee, 23, 137
Boone, Pat, 111, 115
Bouchillon, Chris, 96
Boyd, Eddie, 82, 112, 116, 127, 137
Boyd, Walter, 65
Bradford, Perry, 9-10, 15
Bradley, Will, 50
Bradshaw, Tim, 19
Branch, Billy, 132, 137
Brenston, Jackie, 112-3,
Brewer, James, 126
Brockman, Polk, 67, 95
Broonzy, 'Big Bill', 14, 19, 25, 39, 42, 51-5, 82-3, 96, 124, 126, 132, 137-8
Brown, Alberta, 19
Brown, Charles, 26, 45, 137
Brown, Clarence, 45, 138
Brown, Gabriel, 68
Brown, Gatemouth, 131
Brown, James, 91, 93, 135, 138
Brown, Robert, 54, 63, 138
Brown, Roy, 45, 98, 138

Brown, Ruth, 21, 26, 45, 130, 135, 138
Brown, Washington, 99
Brown, Wilbur C. 74
Brown, Willie, 39, 41, 47-8, 55-6, 59, 69
Bruner, Bill, 98
Brunswick Records, 120
Bruynoghe, Yannick, 124
Bullet Records, 122
Bumble Bee Slim, 51, 138
Bunch, William, 41, 51, 135, 138
Burke, Solomon, 92
Burnett, Chester, 41, 46, 59, 86, 138, 140
Burse, Charlie, 62
Butterfield, Paul, xiv, 84, 117, 119, 138
Byrd, Roy, 45
Byrds, The, 115

California Blues Society, 26
Calloway, Blanche, 130
Calumet Aces, 27
Calvin, Robert, 138
Canned Heat, 48, 99
Cannon, Gus, 39, 61-3, 130, 137-8
Cannon Jug Stompers, 62
Captain Beethart, 99
Carl Lindstrom Co., 9
Carlisle, Una Mae, 20
Carolina Tar Heels, 64
Carr, Barbara, 132
Carr, Leroy, 41-3, 51, 55, 70, 83, 125, 138
Carter, Bo, 60, 122, 138
Carter, Calvin, 117

Carthy, Martin, 126
Carson, John, 40, 96
Castor, Leonard, 33-4, 111
Champion Records, 42
Chance Records, 23, 33
Chapman, Peter, 135, 138, 141
Charles, Ray, 26, 60, 91, 93, 120, 138
Charters, Sam, 38
Chatmon, Armenter, 60, 122, 138
Chatmon, Henderson, 59
Chatmon, Sam, 59, 65, 88
Chauvard, Marcel, 124
Chavis, Wilson, 100
Checker, Chubby, 115
Checker Records, 46, 123
Chenier, C. J., 100, 132, 138
Chenier, Cleveland, 100
Chenier, Clifford, 100
Chenier, Clifton, 138
Chenier, Morris, 100
Chess, Leonard, 83, 88
Chess, Phil, 83
Chess Records, 14, 23, 26, 29-30, 34, 84, 88-9, 98, 113, 118-9
Chevalier, Albert, 101
Chicago Blues Band, 26, 35
Chicago Five, 42, 52
Chitlin Circuit, 75
Chords, 112, 114
Churchill, Savannah, 20
Cincinnati Jug Band, 62-3
Civil War, 4-5
Clapton, Eric, xiv, 26, 31, 45-6, 56, 60, 118, 123, 125
Clayton, Jennie, 63

Clayton, Peter, 32
Clifton, Kaiser, 72
Clovers, 115
Club 51 Records, 33
Cluster, Clay, 79
Coasters, 115
Cobra Records, 33-4, 92-3
Cochran, Eddie, 98
Coleman, Austin, 99
Coleman, Bob, 62-3
Coleman, Jaybird, 40
Collins, Albert, 131-2, 138
Collins, Sam, 41, 59
Columbia Records, 11-2, 15, 20, 34, 42, 44, 50, 55, 63, 73-4, 83, 95-7, 111, 125
Conley, William Lee, 42, 51, 137-8
Connie's Inn, 12
Conqueror Records, 96
Constellation Records, 33
Cooke, Sam, 93
Copeland, James, 93, 138
Copeland, Johnny, 132, 138
Cotton, Elizabeth, 21, 119
Cotton, James, 84, 118, 132, 138
Cox, Ida, xiv, 7-8, 12-3, 16-8, 122, 135, 138
Crawford, Ollie, 111
Crawford, Rosetta, 19
Cray, Robert, 23, 132, 138
Crayton, Pee Wee, 111, 138
Crew Cuts, 112
Crows, 112, 114
Crudup, Arthur, 53, 89, 98, 138
Crump, E. H., 37
Cruthfield, James, 70

Cullen, Anne, 24
Curtis, James, 72

Dago Frank's, 47
Daley, Mayor Richard M., 15
Dallas String Band, 63-4
Darby, Tom, 96
Darin, Bobby, 115
Davenport, Charles, 78-9, 139
Davenport, Jed, 62
Davis, Cyril, 117, 125
Davis, Danny, 97
Davis, Gary, 41, 70, 127, 139
Davis, Jimmie, 96-7
Davis, John, 51, 54, 97
Davis, Maxwell, 120
Davis, Walter, 51, 139
Dawkins, Jimmy, 119, 139
De Berry, James, 72
Decca Records, 24, 44, 48, 98, 111, 125
Delmark Records, 49
Deluxe Records, 23
Demetre, Jacques, 124
Diddley, Bo, 31, 34, 111, 114, 117
Dixieland Jug Band, 61
Dixon, Floyd, 26
Dixon, Willie, xiv, 14-5, 24, 28, 32-5, 84, 88-90, 111, 116-9, 123, 132, 135, 139
Dockery Plantation, 41
Domino, Fats, 111, 114, 117-8
Dominoes, 93, 112
Donigan, Lonnie, 98

Doral, Stanley, 101
Dorsey, Thomas A., 52, 73, 139
Dorsey, Tommy, 50, 97
Douglas, K.C., 70, 139
Douglas, Lizzie, 13
Douglas, Minnie, 139, 141
Doyle, Little Boy, 72
Dreamland Café, 21
Drifters, 46, 112, 115
Dugas, Marcel, 101
Duke Records, 29
Dukes, Laura, 63
Dupree, Jack, 70, 76, 116, 127, 139
Dylan, Bob, 60, 96, 115

Eaglin, Snooks, 70, 139
Easton, Amos, 51, 138
Elko Records, 100
Emancipation Act, 4-5, 102
Empress of the Blues, 11
Estes, John Adams, 41, 48-9, 54, 117, 125, 139
Evans, Elgin, 25
Evans, Ellis, 99
Evans, Margie, 21
Everly Brothers, 98
Ever Ready Gospel Singers, 93
Ezell, Will, 49, 77

Father of Rhythm & Blues, 44
Father of the Blues, 2, 44
Fillmore Circuit, 92
Fisk Jubilee Singers, 5
Fitzgerald, Ella, 19
Five Royales, 91

Fleetwood Mac, xiv, 123
Floyd, Frank, 98, 139
Folk Blues Festival, 117
Folk Festival Circuit, 17
Folkways Records, 24
Fontenot, Conray, 101
Ford, Ernie, 30
Forest, Earl, 29
Foster, Leroy, 25, 82
Fowler, Bernard, 31
Franklin, Aretha, 92-3, 117, 135, 139
Franklin, C.L., 30
Freed, Alan, 113
Fuller, Blind Boy, 41, 69, 98, 137, 139
Fuller, Jesse, 127
Fulson, Lowell, 93, 111, 121, 139

Garlow, Clarence, 100
Garrett, Lloyd, 9
Gaye, Marvin, 115
Gellert, Lawrence, 67
Gennett Records, 20, 62, 97
Georgia Tom, 74-5, 139
Gibson, Cleo, 19
Gillum, William Jazz, 54-5, 97, 139-40
Glinn, Lillian, 18
Glossom, Lonnie, 96
Gold Star Records, 24
Gone Records, 23
Goodman, Benny, 19, 112
Gordon, Robert W., 67
Gordon, Roscoe, 29, 112
Gotham Records, 23
Grace, Teddy, 19
Grant, Coot, 97

Grateful Dead, 60, 62, 99
Gray, Arvella, 47, 126
Grayson, G.B., 98
Green, Lil, 19, 112, 139
Guitar Slim, 99
Guthrie, Woody, 96
Guy, Buddy, 15, 28, 31, 47, 84, 92, 118-9, 123, 139

Hadley, J. J., 59, 139
Haley, Bill, 111, 114
Hall, Roy, 98
Hamfats, Harlem, 52
Hammond, John, 80, 124
Hampton, Lionel, 112
Handy, W.C., xiii, xiv, 2-3, 9, 37, 71-2, 104, 135, 139
Hardin, Lil, 72, 109
Harptones, 46
Harris, Jesse, 69
Harris, Pete, 67
Harris, Wynonie, 98, 139
Hart, Hattie, 63
Hart, John, 99-100
Harvey, Ted, 26
Hatcher, Willie, 54
Hawkins, Coleman, 11, 17
Hayes, Clifford, 61, 63
Headhunters, 25
Hegamin, Lucille, 18, 109, 119
Helfer, Erwin, 70
Hemphill, Jessie Mae, 21, 139
Hemphill, Sid, 63
Henderson, Fletcher, 8, 11, 20, 139
Henderson, Rosa, 10, 139

Hendrix, Jimi, 93, 117-8, 131
Hensley, Larry, 97
Herald Records, 24
Heritage Records, 67
Hicks, Charlie, 74
Hicks, Robert, 74, 137, 139
Hightone Records, 132
Hill, Chippie, 9, 140
Hill, Z.Z., 93, 140
Hines, Earl 'Fatha', 61
Hite, Les, 44
Holcomb, Roscoe, 64
Holiday, Billie, 19, 131, 140
Holly, Buddy, 114
Hopkins, Sam 'Lightnin', 24, 39, 45, 70, 127, 131, 140
Hooker, Earl, 32, 84, 119
Hooker, John Lee, xiv, 22-5, 39, 45, 117-9, 123, 127, 137, 140
Hoover, Herbert, 75
Horton, Walter, 84, 118, 140
Hot Harlem Revue, 20
Eddie 'Son' House, xiv, 22, 41, 43, 45, 47, 55-6, 59, 69, 84, 88, 116, 125, 130, 140
House Rockers, 34
How Come Revue, 20
Howard, Camille, 20
Howell, 'Peg Leg', 74, 122, 140
Hughes, Jimmy, 117
Humes, Helen, 19, 119
Hunter, Alberta, xiv, 7, 12, 19-20, 47, 72, 119, 124, 140
 Hunter, Ivory Joe, 69

Hurt, John, 38, 117, 127, 140
Hutchinson, Frank, 40, 96
Hytone Records, 33

Imperial Records, 45, 131

Jackson, Bessie, 18, 137, 140
Jackson, Bo Weevil, 41, 59
Jackson, Jim, 38, 140
Jackson, John, 70, 140
Jackson, Monroe, 98
Jackson, Papa Charlie, 38, 40, 60-1, 140
Jackson, Vasti, 132, 140
Jacobs, Little Walter, 46, 122, 140
Jagger, Mick, 26, 32
Jake, Shakey, 119
James, Elmore, 28, 88, 93, 122, 140
James, Etta, 30, 119, 130, 140
James, Nehemiah 'Skip' 55, 76, 130, 140
Jax Records, 24
Jazz Age, 73
Jefferson Airplanes, 99, 115
Jefferson, Blind Lemon, 38, 40, 49, 60, 64-5, 68, 73, 82, 97, 132, 140
Job Records, 33
John, Johnny, 119
Johnson, James P., 11
Johnson, Jimmie, 69, 140
Johnson, Johnny, 30-1, 140

Johnson, Lonnie, 17, 25, 32-3, 41, 43, 55, 82, 97, 111, 119, 122, 140
Johnson, Merline, 97
Johnson, Ollie, 69
Johnson, Pete, 50, 80
Johnson, Robert, xiii, xiv, 22, 43, 45, 55-7, 70, 84, 88-9, 140
Johnson, Tommy, 39, 41, 59, 87, 140
Johnson, Willie, 89
Jones, Brian, 28
Jones, Coley, 63
Jones, Curtis, 116, 127, 140
Jones, Dennis, 41
Jones, Johnny, 32
Joplin, Janis, 99
Jordan, Louis, 26, 44, 111, 135
Jordan, Luke, 40
Jordan, Steve, 31

Keesee, Howard, 98
Kelly, Jack, 62
King, Albert, 119-20, 140
King, B.B., 15, 26, 29-30, 46, 89, 92, 111-2, 117, 119-22, 131, 135, 140
King, Ben E., 112
King, Freddie, 93, 119, 140
King of the Blues, 55
King of Zydeco Music, 100
King Records, 23
Kirk, Andy, 43
Knight, Gladys, 115
Knowling, Ramson, 19
Koester, Robert, 70
Kooper, Al, 31

Korean War, 29
Korner, Alexis, 117, 125
Krupa, Gene, 97
Ku Klux Klan, 5

Lacey, Willie, 54
Laibley, Arthur, 67
Lane, James A., 24, 141-2
Lang, Eddie, 97
LaRocca, Nick, 1
LaSalle, Denise, 21
Lawler, Earnest, 9, 14
Leake County Revelers, 64
Leake, Lafayette, 32
Ledbetter, Huddie (Leadbelly) 38, 40, 49, 65, 67, 69, 81-2, 96, 99, 124-6, 132, 141
Lee, Johnny, 23, 141
Lee, Lovie, 120
Lee, Peggy, 19, 112
Lee, Rosa, 96
Lenoir, J.B., 127, 141
Letterman, David, 15
Lewis, Jerry Lee, 98, 114, 117
Lewis, Jimmy, 99
Lewis, Meade 'Lux', 69, 78-80
Lewis, Noah, 61
Lewis, Pete, 111
Lewis, Walter 'Furry', xiv, 37-9, 72, 130, 141
Liggins, Joe, 26, 141
Lincoln, Abraham, 4
Lincoln, Charley, 74
Lincoln Theater, 17
Lipscomb, Mance, 40, 70, 117, 141
Little Richard, 93, 99, 111, 114
Little Walter, 25-7, 33-4, 84, 122, 141
Lockwood, Robert, 46, 57, 72, 87, 123, 126, 141
Lofton, Clarence, 54, 141
Lomax, Alan, 65, 67-9, 83, 95
Lomax, John, 65, 67-9, 82, 95, 99,
Lomax, John Jr., 70
London Palladium, 21
Louis, Joe, 34
Louis, Joe Hill, 46
Love, Jasper, 127
Love, John, 98
Lowry, James, 70
Luandrew, Albert, 32, 141

McClennan, Tommy, 55, 88, 141
McClinton, Delbert, 132, 141
McCoy, Charlie, 97
McCoy, Clyde, 16
McCoy, Joe, 14, 19
McCoy, Memphis Minnie, 7, 9, 13-4, 19-20, 25, 62, 72, 82, 131-2, 139, 141
McCoy, Robert Lee, 54
McCoy, Viola, 10
McDowell, Fred, 117, 141
McGee, Jack, 12
McGhee, Brownie, 40, 96, 116, 124, 127
McGhee, Kirk, 98
McMurray, Lillian, 89
McPhatter, Clyde, 93

McTell, Willie, 68, 70, 74, 141
Mack, Ida May, 8
Macon, Dave, 40
Madison Slim, 26
Magic Sam, 47, 92-3, 119, 122, 141
Maghett, Sam, 47, 122, 141
Magness, Tommy, 98
Malcolm, Horace, 54
Mamas and the Papas, 115
Martha and the Vandellas, 115
Martin, Sarah, 8, 10, 12, 16
Massaro, Salvatore, 97
Mattis, James, 29
Mayall, John, 117, 125
Mayfield, Percy, 93, 120-1, 135, 141
Melotone Records, 62
Melrose, Frank, 97
Melrose, Lester, 83
Memphis Jug Band, 62
Memphis Slim, 30, 34, 76, 82-3, 88, 116, 118, 123, 125, 127, 130, 135, 138, 141
Mercury Records, 33, 98
Merriweather, 'Big Maceo', 25, 28, 51, 141
Midnighters, 114
Miller, Emmett, 97
Millinder, Lucky, 19, 21
Minatures, 28
Miracle Records, 34
Mississippi Sheiks, 59, 63, 88
Miss Rhythm, 21
Modem Records, 26
Modern Records, 23, 122

Monarch Saloon, 71
Monroe, Bill, 98
Montgomery, 'Little Brother', 32-3, 51, 76, 126, 141
Montreux Jazz Festival, 100
Moonglows, 112
Moonshine Kate, 96
Morgan, Richard, 12
Morganfield, McKinley, 45, 69, 82, 141
Morse, Ella Mae, 50
Morton, Benny, 43
Morton, Jelly Roll, 2, 103, 109, 142
Mother of the Blues, 8, 74
Moses Stokes Minstrels, 10
Moss, Buddy, 41, 142
Mr. Magnificent, 26
Music Masters Records, 31
Musselwhite, Charlie, 119, 142

Narmore, Willie T., 98
Neal, Kenny, 132, 142
Nelson, Arnett, 54
Nelson, Ricky, 115
Nelson, Romeo, 76, 79
Nelson, Willie, 97
Newport Folk Festivals, 49, 127
Nicholls, Muriel, 19
Nighthawk, Robert, 25, 34, 82, 119-20, 122, 141-2
Nix, Willie, 29
Nixon, Hammie, 48, 125
Norris, Chuck, 120

Okeh Records, 9, 14-7, 20, 38, 42, 44, 60, 62-3, 95-8, 111
Oliver, King, 17, 109
Oliver, Paul, 126-7
Olssom, Bengt, 125
Opera Records, 33
Original Dixieland Jazz Band, 1
Orioles, 112
Oscher, Paul, 84
Otis, Johnny, 20, 93, 112

Palace Theater, 29, 72
Paramount Records, 8, 16, 18, 37, 39, 49, 60-5, 73, 76, 97, 122
Parker, Little Junior, 47, 120, 142
Park's Big Revue, 10
Parlophone Records, 124
Patton, Bill,C., 59
Patton, Charley, xiii, xiv, 22, 38-9, 41, 43, 55-6, 58-60, 86-8, 135, 139, 142
Peacock Records, 20
Penquins, 46, 114-5
Perkins, Carl, 98
Perkins, Joe, 72
Petway, Robert, 55
Phillips, Esther, 93
Piano Willie, 26
Picaninny Jug Band, 62
Pickett, Wilson, 93
Pierce, Billie, 70
Pitre, Wild Bill, 101
Platters, 114
Presley, Elvis, 20, 30, 63, 98, 111-2, 114

Prestige Records, 32
Pridgett, Gertrude, 8, 142
Prime, Alberta, 20
Pryor, Snooky, 25, 142

Queen of the Blues, 14-5, 131
Queen Mother of the Blues, 130
Queen of Soul, 92

Rabbit Foot Minstrels, 8, 11, 47
Rachell, Yank, 48, 125, 142
Rainey, Gertrude 'Ma', xiv, 3, 8-13, 16-20, 33, 74, 130, 132, 135, 142
Rainey, William 'Pa', 8
Raitt, Bonnie, 21, 23, 28, 135
Ramblers, Hackberry, 60
Ramsey, Frederic Jr. 69
Rawls, Lou, 120
Ray, Johnny, 111
Redding, Otis, 93
Red Hot Louisiana Band, 100
Redman, Don, 11
Reed, Jimmy, 47, 117-8, 142
Regal Records, 33
Regent Records, 23
Rhythm & Blues, 122, 129
Richards, Keith, 26, 31, 56, 126
Ringling Brothers Circus, 13
Riverside Records, 23
Robertson, Eck, 96
Robeson, Paul, 21

Robey, Don, 29
Robinson, Fenton, 132, 142
Robinson, James, 70
Rock 'n' Roll, 122
Rock 'n' Roll Hall of Fame, 21, 23, 30, 43, 45-6, 122, 131
Rodgers, Jesse, 98
Rodgers, Jimmy, 84, 87-8, 96-7, 135, 142
Rogers, Jimmy, 24-6, 39, 45, 84, 99, 141-2
Rogers, Jimmy, Jr., 26
Rolling Stones, 28, 32, 34, 46, 56, 88, 115, 117, 122-3, 125-6, 131
Rooftop Singers, 63
Roosevelt, Franklin D., 51-2
Ross, Bertha, 19
Roulette, Freddie, 119
Royals, 93
RPM Records, 122
Rubin, Alton, 99
Rush, Otis, 31, 92-3, 119, 142
Rushing, Jimmy, 40, 142
Russell, William, 69

Sane, Dan, 37, 39
Santana, Carlos, 23, 28, 118
Sapps, Booker T., 68
Saunders, Gertrude, 124
Savoy Records, 23, 112
Scott, Shirley, 120
Sebastian, John, 31
Seeger, Pete, 70
Shade, Will, 62-3, 127
Shaffer, Paul, 15
Shaw, Allen, 72
Shaw, Robert, 117
Shines, Johnny, 31, 119, 142
Short, J.D., 59
Showboat, 21
Simeone, Henry, 19
Sims, Frank Lee, 45, 142
Singing Bartender, 43
Slack, Freddie, 50
Sledge, Percy, 93
Slim, Memphis, 30, 34, 76, 82-3, 116, 118, 123, 125, 127, 130, 135, 138, 141
Sloan, Henry, xiv
Smith, Arthur, 98
Smith, Bessie, xiv, 7-13, 15-20, 97, 124, 130, 132, 135, 142
Smith, 'Big Maybelle', 45
Smith, Casey, 68
Smith, Clara, 8, 10, 12, 19, 135, 142
Smith, Clarence, 79, 142
Smith, Hugh, Dr., 13
Smith, Mamie, xiv, 7, 9-13, 15-7, 47, 109-10, 132, 142
Smith, Robert Curtis, 127
Smith, Shellie, 98
Smith, Trixie, 16, 142
Smith, Willie, 24
Snow, Phoebe, 31
Son Seals, 132, 142
Spand, Charlie, 73, 77
Spann, Otis, 28, 84, 118, 122, 124, 126, 143
Specialty Records, 120
Speckled Red, 70, 75, 77
Speir, H. C., 67
Spinners, 115
Spivey, Addie (SweetPease), 19

Spivey, Victoria, 13, 17-8, 40, 64-5, 119, 143
Staff Records, 23
Stafford, Mary, 19
Starr, Kay, 112
Stax Records, 120
Stokes, Frank, 37, 135, 143
Storyville Records, 126
Stroger, Bob, 26
Strothers, Jimmie, 68
Sumlin, Hubert, 89, 143
Sun Records, 98
Sunnyland Slim, xiv, 24-5, 28, 32-3, 82-3, 119, 126, 141
Sunny Records, 33
Supreme Records, 120
Supremes, 93, 115
Swan Records, 16
Sweetheart of Dreamland, 21
Swing-Time Records, 44
Sykes, Roosevelt, 51, 57, 76, 82, 126, 143
Sylvester, Hannah, 21, 119

Tampa Red, 14, 25, 27-8, 39, 42-3, 52-3, 55, 74, 82-3, 132, 143
Tarlton, Jimmie, 96
Taylor, Arthur 'Momtana', 79, 143
Taylor, Eddie, 47, 119, 143
Taylor, Koko, 14-5, 118-9, 135, 143
Taylor, Robert, 14
Taylor, Walter, 62
Temptations, 93
Terrell, Saunders, 41
Terrell, Sonny, 40, 123, 143

Terry, Sonny, 41, 69, 96, 116, 124, 127
Texas Slim, 23
Tharpe, Rosetta, Sister, 19, 142
Theater Owner's Booking Association, 15, 72
Thomas, Henry, 36, 143
Thomas, Hociel, 19, 143
Thomas, Willard, 41
Thomas, Willie, 70
Thompson, Ashley, 61
Thornton, Willie Mae, (Big Mama), xiv, 20, 45, 112, 143
Ticker, Luther, 119
Tomato Records, 132
Townsend, Henry, 64, 143
Trevellian, Henry, 69
Trilon Records, 121
Trumpet Records, 89
Tubbs, Ernest, 30
Tucker, Bessie, 9, 18
Turner, Ike, xiv, 29, 89, 93
Turner, Joseph Vernon, 43-4, 51, 111, 114, 119, 135, 137, 143
Turner, Tina, 93

Uncrowned Queen of the Blues, 16

Van Halen, Eddie, xiv, 118
Vaughn, Sarah, 20, 143
Vaughn, Stevie Ray, 118
Vee Jay Records, 31, 33, 117-8
Victor Records, 19-20, 33, 41-2, 44, 48, 50, 53, 61-2, 73, 83, 96-8, 111, 120

Vincent, Gene, 9
Vinson, Eddie, 45, 143
Vocalion Records, 14, 36, 38, 41, 43-4, 48, 50-1, 59, 73, 97-8

Walker, Frank, 11, 67, 95-6
Walker, Jimmy, 132
Walker, Little, 30
Walker, T-Bone, 24, 40, 44-5, 65, 111, 119, 123, 131, 143
Wallace, Beulah 'Sippie', 7, 17, 124, 143
Waller, Fats, 20
Walter, Little, 32, 143
Walton, Cora, 14, 143
Walton, Wade, 127
Wand, Hart, 9,
Wander Inn Cafe, 12
Ward, Billy, 93, 112
Washboard Band, 63
Washboard Rhythm Kings, 63
Washboard Sam, 54-5, 63, 97, 138, 143
Washboard Serenaders, 63
Washboard Trio, 62
Washington, Dinah, 20, 120
Waters, Ethel, 18, 124
Waters, Muddy, xiv, 22, 24, 26-8, 30, 32-4, 39, 45, 55, 57, 69, 81, 83-9, 111, 118, 124, 132, 141
Watson, Doc, 60
Watson, Johnny, 40
Weather Report, 11
Weinberg, Max, 31
Weldon, 'Casey Bill', 14, 144

Wellington, Valerie, 21
Wells, Junior, 14-5, 24, 27, 84, 92, 118, 137, 144
Wells, Viola, 21, 119
Weston, Ruth, 21, 138
Wheatstraw, Peetie, 41, 43, 51, 135, 138, 144
White, Bukka, 39, 41, 48, 55, 68, 117, 121, 144
White, George, L., 5, 19
White, Joshua, 122, 144
White, Leroy, 'Lasses', 9
White, Lynn, 21, 144
White, Marva, 132
WhiteTrash Horns, 28
Whittaker, Hudson, 52, 74, 143
Who, The, 123
Williams, 'Big Joe', xiv, 39, 47, 54, 57, 70, 121
Williams, Bill, 40
Williams, Clarence, 11
Williams, Hank, 40
Williams, Henry, 74
Williams, Johnny, 23, 144
Williams, Robert Pete, 117, 144
Williamson, 'Big Joe', 123
Williamson, John Lee, (Sonny Boy), 28, 30-1, 33-4, 51, 54-5, 57, 82-3, 88, 117-8, 121-2, 144
Williamson, Robert Pete, 70
Williamson, 'Sonny Boy' 'Rice', 25, 27, 72, 87, 89-90, 123, 126, 144
Willington, Valerie, 47
Wilson, Al, 48
Wilson, Edith, 10, 19, 119

www.ingramcontent.com/pod-product-compliance
Lightning Source LLC
LaVergne TN
LVHW051556070426
835507LV00021B/2605

9 780934 687430